PATHS & F

Nigel Heath & Peter Gibbs

ISBN: 9798362555566

Our grateful thanks to all who have helped us on our way over the last four decades, including my wife, Jenny, and Peter's late partner, Sally, as well as countless others, who have freely shared advice, offered directions and showed us numerous acts of kindness as we walked 4,000 miles on footpaths, waterways and canal towpaths.

CONTENTS

SETTING OFF...7

THE WALKS:

THE COLERIDGE WAY..............................10

THE COVENTRY CANAL............................18

THE CROSS BRITAIN WAY.........................25

THE GRAND UNION & SHROPSHIRE UNION CANALS....44

THE HEART OF ENGLAND WAY..............51

THE HUDDERSFIELD NARROW CANAL...................63

THE LEEDS & LIVERPOOL CANAL..........................69

THE LLANGOLLEN CANAL.....................................85

THE MACMILLAN WAY..93

THE OXFORD CANAL...111

THE OXFORDSHIRE WAY.....................................117

THE SEVERN WAY..123

SHAKESPEARE'S AVON WAY...............................129

SHAKESPEARE'S WAY...137

THE SOUTHERN COAST-TO-COAST......................143

THE STAFFORDSHIRE & WORCESTERSHIRE
CANAL...152

THE STRATFORD CANAL......................................162

THE TEST WAY..168

THE THAMES PATH..175

THE TRENT & MERSEY CANAL.............................196

THE AMTRAK RAIL JOURNEYS:.............................206

THE CALIFORNIA ZEPHYR...............................207

THE TEXAS EAGLE..220

THE OTHER WAYS...235

MORE TALES FROM THE TRAILS........................239

JOURNEY'S END – FOR NOW..............................243

USEFUL INFORMATION.....................................247

THE POEMS:

WHEN RAIN BECAME TRAIN.................................8

AUTUMN FALLS...16

LUCKY MONEY TREE..17

CANAL KALEIDOSCOPE......................................22

OLD TRUNK SEAT...23

LONELY HEART..24

CROSSING BRITAIN...40

GOLDEN WEEDS...42

MOST UNCOMMON BLUE......................................43

A CANAL LABELLED GRAND..................................49

CATHEDRAL CHORUS..59

HS2 VIEW..60

SPINDLEBERRY DAY...61

PUMPKIN SPREE...62

PENNINES DIVIDED..67

TUNNEL VISION..68

WALKING THE CANAL..82

DRY REQUISITE TROUSERS............................83

SCARLET RAIN...84

APRIL CANAL WALKING...................................90

CANAL CRISS-CROSS....................................91

NATURE'S PICTURE PATCHWORK......................106

BAUNTON IN JANUARY.................................109

CROPREDY MEAL...116

CRISS-CROSSING HISTORY.............................122

SEVERN SOURCE TO SILVER SEA....................127

SHAKESPEARE'S WAY WITH THE AVON.............136

WALKING WITH WILLIAM................................142

SNOWFALL IN SELBORNE...............................150

SCARPA BOOTS...151

TOWPATH IN WINTER...................................159

STRIDING TO STRATFORD..............................167

PASSING THE TEST.......................................173

FEEDING AN ILLUSION..................................174

MEN OF STEEL..193

SEEKING THE SOURCE..................................194

WALKING THE TRENT & MERSEY......................205

THE CALIFORNIA ZEPHYR...............................212

THE TEXAS EAGLE.......................................225

BOOTS AWAY..244

SETTING OFF

"I'm having some disloyal thoughts," my life-long walking companion, Peter, admitted.

It was around mid-day. We'd spent a miserable morning walking Scotland's famous West Highland Way in relentless pouring rain and were now sitting at the back of a forlorn campsite under a tree having a coffee break.

"What are they?" I asked as another raindrop from a dripping branch plopped into my flask cup.

He replied: "The railway station's over there, we've been on the trail for two days, so why don't we stop right here and now, take the train into Fort William and come back in the Spring to complete the walk?"

We were two novice walkers on our first long-distance trail adventure and were so green that neither of us had realised that our brand-new rucksacks were not waterproof and required liners.

The weather had been glorious the day before as we walked along the side of stunningly-picturesque Loch Lomond.

But after an overnight stop in Crianlarich it changed with a vengeance and by the time we arrived at that campsite near Tyndrum everything in our rucksacks, which our inexperience had also led us to overfill, was beyond damp and would need drying.

I did not take any persuading, so on arriving in Fort William, we booked into a hotel, draped all our soggy clothes over the radiators in our room and went out for a consolation supper at a waterfront restaurant.

By complete chance, a family on a touring holiday, whom we'd met that morning 50-plus miles away in Crianlarich, were also there. "My, you've made good time!" they exclaimed.

WHEN RAIN BECAME TRAIN

Oh, listen, all ye walkers
And harken to my tale
Of what befell two brave young lads
Who travelled North by rail
It was their first time trekking
The route – West Highland Way
With hopes and inexperience
They launched their brave foray
The trip began at Temple Meads
With biscuits and a drink
Their train arrived at Platform Three
Within an eyelid's blink
The cabin staff were first class
The sleeper berths a dream
They breakfasted on salmon smoked
And coffee laced with cream
Beyond the window laid displayed
A sunlit Scottish scene
With snow-capped mountains far away
And lochs and burns between
At Glasgow Central they'd agreed
To skip a boring bit
Went on to start at Ardlui
Alighting feeling fit
Loch Lomond was before them
'Neath skies all blue, not grey,
They strolled along those bonnie banks
And sunshine blessed the day
Next morn the weather worsened
They trudged in pouring rain
And their resolve just weakened
At Tyndrum with a train
That took them on to Fort William
With views of might have been
A sorrier pair of trekkers
Were never, ever seen.

It's now over forty years since Peter had that disloyal thought and we have been walking the highways and byways of England and Wales ever since - up hill and down dale, across open and wooded country, following river banks and coastal paths and along canals.

And while I write the words, Peter pens a poem when inspired by the places visited on the walk or the beauty of nature along the way.

This story really begins when I was a district reporter covering North Somerset for the then Bristol Evening Post and Peter was assistant editor with the sister paper, the Western Daily Press.

We both had young families and met at a party hosted by a colleague in the Victorian seaside town of Clevedon.

"Do you fancy going for a walk, Peter?" I asked and the rest as they say is history.

We are now both in our seventies, have crossed the country four times, covering some four thousand miles, and continue to take inspiration from an indomitable lady, well into her eighties, who we met on the trail one day.

"What keeps you going?" Peter asked. "It's keeping going that keeps me going, young man!" came her instant reply.

THE COLERIDGE WAY
Nether Stowey to Lynmouth – 51 miles

"I wonder what adventures we shall have today," I said to Peter as we set out from a picturesque Somerset village on a stormy autumn morning.

It was the ritual question I always ask at the start of our latest long-distance trek.

This time we were following in the footsteps of one of England's most famous poets, Samuel Taylor Coleridge, from his cottage in Nether Stowey, all the way to Lynmouth in North Devon.

Had I known the answer to my question, I am not sure I would have quite believed it.

For during the course of that first day on the Coleridge Way, we met a dinosaur, stared up at white clouds of cotton wool and came across a world-famous church gargoyle.

The huge wrought iron dinosaur put in an early appearance, as he was guarding a villager's garden, just before we began our long climb up the wooded slopes of the Quantock Hills.

The heavens opened after we gained the ridge only to discover that the way now led back down wooded Holford Combe, almost to sea level, before climbing back up again past Alfoxton House, once rented for a season by Coleridge's fellow Romantics poet, William Wordsworth, and his sister, Dorothy, and where he was a regular visitor.

Then, as we regained the height, we were rewarded by magnificent views across the Bristol Channel to Wales.

By lunchtime, we'd crossed back over the Quantock ridge to descend to the pretty village of Bicknoller and then on to the quaintly-named village of Monksilver, where we were overnighting, and it was here that the rest of the day's memorable adventures began.

We'd made good time and were hoping for a late afternoon pint in the Notley Arms, but being a Monday, the hostelry was closed.

"Never mind, Pete, as it's a bit too early to go to the B&B, let's just sit outside the pub and have a breather." I said, which turned out to be a most fortunate suggestion.

For five minutes later, the landlord appeared and, to our surprise, invited us in.

We'd not been settled with our pints long before Peter looked up to see a cluster of white cotton wool clouds suspended from the ceiling - so what on earth was all that about? we wondered.

The ingenious explanation, the landlord told us, was that because the bar and restaurant areas had stone floors, this produced too much additional noise when there were a lot of customers in.

11

So the fluffy clouds were designed to absorb the sound and were a bit like the much larger mushroom-shaped ones used in the roof of a packed Royal Albert Hall.

The landlord then gave us a mini-local history lesson, including the fascinating fact that adorning the nearby parish church was a gargoyle, believed to be the first of its kind in the world, because it depicted a dentist with his patient.

So, we had to go and check this out and, sure enough, there they were together with a pot of ale to anaesthetise the patient.

The following morning, we trudged uphill on a footpath through oak woodland for a mile and a quarter en route for our next stop in the hamlet of Luxborough.

Shortly afterwards, we were chatting as we walked along a narrow lane, when we heard a vehicle behind us and turned to meet a Forestry England Wildlife Ranger, who has kept watch across Exmoor and the neighbouring Quantock and Blackdown Hills for the past thirty years.

These days he spends much of his time protecting wild life habitats, while liaising with contractors coming in to harvest the timber.

"They might need to be aware of particularly sensitive areas, where we may have anything from dormice, birds and bats to other wildlife habitats to protect," he explained.

With four miles to walk, we stopped for lunch at The Valiant Soldier in Roadwater, where the landlord said his business had definitely benefited from having the Coleridge Way running past his front door.

He told how during the last war, the local Home Guard came up with the cunning plan of disguising a pill box as a house, which we had to go and check out.

We stayed overnight in Luxborough's comfortable Royal Oak before setting out on the next 13-mile hike to the picturesque town of Porlock on the shores of the Bristol Channel.

En route, we crossed open moorland, close to the mighty Dunkery Beacon, the highest point on Exmoor, and then on to Webber's Post, above the wooded coombes of pretty Horner Water.

Now we descended through woodland to the hamlet of Horner, where I was delighted to see that the tea garden, which I first visited over 30 years ago, is still going strong.

Refreshed by tea and cake, it was then only a short woodland stroll into Porlock for our overnight stop.

The final day of the walk from Porlock to Lynmouth was all about a very steep hill, a famous romantic story, and what has to be one of the prettiest waterside woodland walks in Britain, plus a final surprise!

The hill is Porlock Hill, so long and steep that even the guide book advises Coleridge Way walkers to have a day's rest before tackling it.

The path winds its way up through woodland to pass tiny Culbone Church, the smallest in England, via a small detour, and then eventually over the busy A39 Lynmouth road to drop down to the little church at Oare, close to the famous Doone Valley.

It was here in R.J. Blackmore's famous novel, Lorna Doone, that the heroine was shot, but recovered.

Later, the way arrives at the tiny hamlet of Brendon to meet the fast-flowing East Lyn River, which it follows all the way down to Lynmouth via tiny Rockford and the famous Watersmeet beauty spot.

But close to journey's end, we came across a fallen trunk pitted with hundreds of coins.

Apparently, these 'Money Trees,' have randomly popped up all over the country in recent years and supposedly bring donors prosperity and good luck
.

I found a place for a shiny ten pence piece, but as I walked away, it occurred to me that we'd already been lucky enough to enjoy four days' walking through wonderful scenery cloaked in autumn's gold.

Guide book: The Coleridge Way Companion Guide - www.coleridgewaywalk.co.uk/

AUTUMN FALLS

Water rushing downwards
From off encircling hills
As beneath the rock face
The small brook quickly fills
Oak trees that Tudor Navy
Made masts both straight and true
A steep path heading upwards
As early light shines through
Acorns in abundance
'Twixt leaves of brown and gold
While out across the red-earth fields
The misty views unfold
A wide track leading westward
Beneath a line of beech
Towards a wooded skyline
With Exmoor now in reach

Ancient trunks embedded
In layered banks of flint
Along the lovely bridleway
That bears the horses' print
Autumn on the Coleridge Way
With thoughts of poets past
Colours there at every turn
Weave memories that will last.

LUCKY MONEY TREE

In these times when Covid
Has hit economy
How wonderful to know there is
A real life money tree
You'll find it close to Lynmouth
Just down from Watersmeet
Where river flows so swiftly
And near a handy seat
The trunk it might seem normal
But then springs a surprise
For in its bark are countless coins
Of each and every size
It might not save our nation
But if we're really stuck
Some coinage freely given here
May bring much-needed luck.

THE COVENTRY CANAL
Fradley Junction to Coventry – 38 miles

Peter and I had not been sent to Coventry because we were willingly walking there along a wonderfully rural waterway linking the city with the mighty Trent and Mersey Canal.

It was while we were trekking that other canal on a glorious June afternoon that we first came upon the Fradley Junction with the Coventry Canal and wondered what future adventures that waterway might provide.

So now we had returned early on a cold and crisp November morning under crystal clear blue skies to trek the thirty-eight miles into Coventry.

The rising sun shining directly into our faces, set the canal-side trees ablaze, casting a golden glow over the millions of autumn leaves carpeting the path ahead and floating on the still waters below.

The Coventry Canal was constructed between 1768 and 1789 to give the rapidly-expanding city access to wider markets and to exploit the potential of the Warwickshire coalfields.

Today it is a magnet for narrowboat enthusiasts and it seemed that this sunny morning had tempted shoals of them out from their moorings to cruise the waterway, casting a myriad of reflections as they passed.

Sitting on the stern of his narrowboat, we came upon a retired Somerset tree surgeon, who had roamed far and wide around the waterways over recent years.

He was preparing to make soup and a risotto from a locally-grown pumpkin left over from Halloween and would soon be off to a nearby farm for a large jug of milk.

"Members of the local narrowboat fraternity enjoy a real community spirit and that's what I love about this life," he said, stopping to greet another skipper passing by.

The late afternoon shadows were lengthening as we reached the small canal-side town of Fazely, where we were staying for the night.

We were made most welcome at the inn and after a pleasant evening, an excellent supper and a good night's rest, we left Fazely under cold and overcast skies, soon to cross a wide reach of the River Tame, a major tributary of the River Trent.

By 11am we were ready for a coffee break and soon came upon a seat made from a fallen tree trunk, the perfect spot facing the sun.

Shortly afterwards, we noticed there was a collection of personal mementos pinned to a nearby tree and we wondered what that was all about.

We had not long set off again when we met an elderly lady walking towards us and we asked her if she knew the answer to our question.

"Yes, I do," she replied. "When my late husband was in poor health, we used to walk as far as that seat, so after he sadly died, my family decided to commemorate our much-loved spot."

By noon we'd reached Polesworth and ventured into The Bulls Head, where we received a warm welcome from a group of locals already partaking in some good crack.

This small village was renowned in the 16th Century as the largest literary gathering outside London and its history is now marked by the Polesworth Poetry Trail.

That afternoon before heading out into open country with some fine views of distant hills, we came upon a contractor's barge with its three-man crew.

They were busy cutting and chipping overhanging branches to keep the waterway clear on behalf of the Canal and River Trust, which employs teams doing essential maintenance work around the network during the winter months.

Reaching the bustling canal-side town of Atherstone, where we were overnighting at the Red Lion Hotel, we treated ourselves to a large pot of tea with cake in the former coaching inn's comfortable lounge.

Early the following morning, we quickly came upon the impressive Atherstone flight of eleven locks, which, covering two miles, lift the waterway eighty feet above the Leicestershire plain.

Not far beyond, we reached Hartshill, lying within the old Roman settlement of Mancetter, and it was believed to be here in AD 60 that a highly-disciplined Roman legion completely destroyed Boudicca's 80,000-strong rebel army, whereupon the Iceni heroine took poison.

The canal now weaved its way for miles around the edge of higher ground with some fine views towards open country below.

We were passing through an area, where extensive quarrying provided millions of tonnes of granite and quartz traffic for the canal.

One highly-visible reminder of those industrial days is Mount Jud, a conical mountain of rock spoil rising 426-feet above sea level and named after the quarry-owning Judkins family.

Passing through the outskirts of Nuneaton, we were quickly out into open country again and soon to have a literary surprise.

For diverting off the canal and walking a mile along a country lane, we came upon Griff House, now a Premier Inn and Beefeater Restaurant, but formerly the home of Victorian author George Eliot, who lived there until she was twenty-one.

The sun was just rising over the horizon into a clear blue sky as we regained the canal the following morning for our final eight-mile walk to the canal basin in the heart of Coventry.

After passing the quiet Marston Junction with the Ashby Canal, we came upon on the far-more-important Hawkesbury Junction with the Oxford Canal, which we'd walked some years earlier.

The Coventry and Oxford canals share the distinction of being the two oldest in the country.

Not far from journey's end we came upon a group of the Canal and River Trust's Coventry Five and A Half Towpath Task Force volunteers.

Covering the canal from the Coventry Basin to Hawkesbury Junction, they carry out general maintenance tasks, including towpath repairs and litter picking.

Surprisingly, the canal remains a green and pleasant walk right into the heart of the city and there at the end of the towpath was a cafe.

Looking back on the walk over an early lunch, we pondered over the many sights we had seen along the way, including a large white love heart with two pictures of the Eiffel Tower.

But what romantic story that had to tell, I guess we shall never know.

Guide book: J.M. Pearson's Canal Companion: South Midlands - www.jmpearson.co.uk/

CANAL KALEIDOSCOPE

Frost upon the towpath
A golden light's reflection
Illuminates a dawning day
That promises perfection
Canal a placid ribbon
'Tween avenue of trees
Its surface a kaleidoscope
Of multi-coloured leaves
Cleaving through the silence
A narrowboat moves by
Smoke from out its silver stack
Ascending to the sky.

THE OLD TRUNK SEAT

Beside the sunlit calm canal
Cool shaded by tall trees
A seat from old trunk fashioned
A place to take one's ease
In peaceful contemplation
As narrow boats pass by
Beyond the fields of buttercups
Beneath a clear blue sky
Flag iris in profusion
Bright yellow paints the way
Lining the quiet waters
Where commerce once held sway.

LONELY HEART

A pierced heart on a lonely tree
Beside quiet waterway
Its meaning just a mystery
As walkers briefly stay
Two images of Paris
Fill wooden frames of white
Perhaps a sad reminder
Of lovers lost from sight
The Eiffel Tower a beacon
That shone across the years
Memories of romance past
Recalled now just with tears.

THE CROSS BRITAIN WAY
Boston to Barmouth – 280 miles

"We're on the road again," I said to Peter as we stood with our backs to Boston's famous 'Stump' church tower early on a chilly November morning.

Ahead lay four wonderful days walking to escape the vast flatness of the Lincolnshire fens and on to higher ground as we headed for Margaret Thatcher's home town of Grantham and beyond.

Four further weeks' walking in January, March, April and June would take us through Winter and out into Spring and Summer and so on to the North Wales resort of Barmouth on the Irish Sea.

We were starting a new 280-mile cross-Britain trail created by the Macmillan Way Association, as a sequel to their now extremely-popular long-distance trek from Boston to Abbotsbury, Dorset, which we had completed years earlier.

"I wonder what adventures we'll have along the way?" I remarked, as we hoisted our packs onto our backs, took up our walking poles and set forth, soon to pass a cluster of fishing boats on the banks of the River Witham estuary.

They were the final echo of the 13th Century, when Boston rivalled London for trade with Northern Europe.

And strangely enough it was beyond Kirton, with its eye-catching metal village sign, that we stopped in a cafe and met a local, now living in the Netherlands, who said how lucky we were to have the legal right to roam.

We decided on lunch in the oddly-named village of Wigtoft, where our trusty Ordnance Survey map told us there was a pub, but it was nowhere to be found.

Then, as if on cue, a council lorry driver arrived to empty the bins and told us the pub had closed some time ago, so it was on to our often-used plan B and sandwiches in the nearby parish church porch.

"There are tables inside," invited a lady, who'd popped in to borrow the church wheelchair.

We got chatting about the state of the world and she told us the silver lining story of how her ambulance driver son had thrice resuscitated a badly-injured tourist on the way to hospital after the London Tube bombings and had later attended her wedding in Australia.

It was time to go and on leaving this quiet village, we crossed the noisy A16 Boston to Spalding road and were soon on a quiet lane in the midst of a dead flat landscape sown with vast swathes of cabbages and Brussels sprouts for as far as the eye could see and all destined for our ravenously-hungry supermarkets.

Further on we spotted a tiny 'Cross Britain Way 'sticker, many hundreds more of which would help guide us safely onwards.

Storm clouds were gathering as we plodded into Donington to meet the statue of Matthew Flinders standing quietly in the market square, holding his telescope with his faithful cat, Trim, at his feet.

This famous explorer was the first to circumnavigate Australia, charting and naming most of the southern coast, including Cape Donington, and we read that there are more statues of him 'Down Under' than any other historic figure, with the exception of Queen Victoria.

The heavens were about to open, so we took refuge in the Black Bull, where we were welcomed by a roaring log fire and a friendly crowd of locals. This was just perfect because our B&B was close by and the pub served evening meals.

Early the next morning, we were back on the trail and again surrounded by vast arrays of crops, as we followed a small lane, which our Cross Britain Way guide book told us would eventually end at the South Forty Foot Drain, which dates back to the 17th Century.

But because we were chatting and I was not paying attention to the map, we went straight ahead on a sharp bend and ended up in a deserted farmyard with no sign of the drain, which is a substantial waterway helping to prevent flooding in The Fens.

It took a few minutes to figure out where we'd gone wrong and to return to the lane, which, in fact, continued for another two miles. It was a sharp reminder that paying attention was preferable to many a wasted step.

The way now led across more vast tracts of open land, through the picturesque villages of Horbling and Billingborough, but the ground started rising as we trudged up the long hill to journey's end in Folkingham.

The spreading rays of sunset turned the church clock face to gold as we found our way to our B&B in a magnificently-converted barn and as luck would have it, there was a village pub serving supper.

The following day, with The Fens now far behind us, we found our way along quiet lanes and country paths, through Sapperton, where we sat for coffee in the churchyard, on to Ropsley and finally to Old Somerby, where we left the trail to walk into busy Grantham for the night.

By a stroke of luck our hotel was opposite the Grantham Canal, along which we walked for five miles the following morning to re-join the trail at Woolsthorpe Wharf.

Journey's end was now in sight and after passing close by Belvoir Castle, now a conference and wedding venue, we left the trail to walk into nearby Redmile, where we'd arranged for a taxi to take us the 60 miles back to Boston.

Cross Britain Way – Part Two

It was to be a day of new beginnings and some sad memories at the start of the second stage of our Cross Britain walk, as we headed out from the Leicestershire village of Redmile on a crisp January morning.

Ahead lay our day's trek along the half-frozen Grantham Canal, where ducks found it difficult to dabble, as it wound its way through the Vale of Belvoir.

As the light was beginning to fade, a dog walker told us there was a new teashop ahead in the canal basin at Hickling, but we'd have to hurry because it closed at 4pm and luckily we made it just in time.

Earlier, we had come across a poignant memorial to the crew of a Lancaster bomber, which crashed while returning from France in 1943.

Six young men died while one survived, but it was heartening to see fresh wreaths laid at the scene after all these years.

We spent the night at a comfortable B&B, having dined at a local pub, and were back on the trail early the following morning and now climbing steadily up a long spur of the rolling Leicestershire Wolds, with magnificent views on either side and another small adventure just ahead.

One feature of winter walking is that most cattle are kept indoors - not that I have ever had the slightest hesitation about walking quietly through grazing cows, but highly-inquisitive and frisky horses, I do find more challenging.

Two such magnificent animals were occupying a small field ahead and I could see they were in a playful mood!

I was quickly over the stile and walking on as they approached, but Peter was not so lucky having to fend off their probing noses as he completed the manoeuvre.

He is far more at ease with horses than I and chatted to them as we passed through their paddock.

A whole series of bright yellow footpath marker posts kept us en route throughout the day, but then a shortage of accommodation forced us to divert from our course to spend the night in the nearby village of Remstone.

Back on the path the following misty morning, we made our way to Normanton-on-Soar and stopped for coffee on a seat in the parish churchyard, close to the rain-swollen river, and here I spotted my first snowdrop of the year.

A watery sun appeared as we crossed the Soar on a series of weir bridges and headed for Hathen, where, early in the 19th Century, the vicar, the Rev March Phillips, became so fed up with the cockfighting and drunken brawling in his churchyard that he declared the village to be a ' wicked place.'

The enticing appeal of a log fire, a couple of pints and a bowl of soup caused us to tarry longer than was prudent in the Plough Inn at Diseworth for which we later paid a heavy price as we laboured uphill and over muddy fields.

A golden sun just above the horizon, and directly ahead, made it difficult to spot the yellow post footpath markers in crossing hedgerows, so it was almost dark when at last we reached a road.

Ahead, where lights were beginning to twinkle, was the historic village of Breedon-on-the-Hill and I cursed 'villages on Breedon hills' as we climbed wearily towards it, but now a rich reward for our day's labours was in store.

Here our overnight stay was at Breedon Hall, a magnificent Georgian mansion, lovingly rescued and restored from an office complex and now a luxury B&B complete with lovely period furnishings.

Our penultimate day on the trail was to prove the most scenic as we climbed to the Iron Age Breedon hill fort with lovely views and descended through fields to Melbourne and its stately lakeside Melbourne Hall.

This was the family seat of William Lamb, Viscount Melbourne, who gave his name to an Australian city and was a young Queen Victoria's first Prime Minister.

From here we walked beside the Staunton Harold reservoir and through woodland to reach the National Trust's massive Calke Abbey House set in acres of estate parkland.

Sitting and leaning against a fence, we feasted in the park on cheesy scones, bought earlier at the reservoir visitor's centre, before following a section of the Robin Hood's Way into the historic market town of Ashby-de-la-Zouch for our final night's stay.

Somewhere just a little further on the way to the village of Coton in the Elms, we would be completing our first 100 miles.

Cross Britain Way – Part Three

It was coffee time and Peter and I were strolling along a sunny country lane near the Derbyshire village of Rosliston, when I spotted a field entrance set back in deep shade.

No sooner had we shed our heavy packs and were leaning against its gate with flask cups in hand when a family drove up to move their horses!

Hazard lights flashed and belongings were scattered as we scrambled to clear the way for which we were rewarded by being invited to finish our so-rudely-interrupted break inside their field.

The Cosmic Joker, our unseen companion, who we feel sometimes upsets the best laid plans, had struck yet again!

On reaching Walton-on-Trent, an attractive village of red brick houses, that Sunday lunchtime, we picnicked in the grounds of St Laurence Church, before crossing a bridge over the River Trent to enter Staffordshire.

Peter paused to take a picture, and as he did so, three paddle boarders popped out from under the Bailey Bridge structure and into his frame.

After crossing another old friend, the Trent and Mersey Canal, our route now led into a bustling water park, where hundreds of families were making the most of the sunshine, but luckily the path was quickly leading us away from this throng.

However, Peter fancied afternoon tea, which meant an unpleasant diversion through a packed car park only to find that the teashop was closed. Another successful strike for our Cosmic Joker!

Half an hour later, we strolled wearily into Barton-under-Needwood with its many fine old buildings to stop overnight at The Shoulder of Mutton, whose proprietors were most welcoming.

Refreshed, we set out on a wonderful Monday walk through the South Staffordshire countryside, where fields of rape seed stood out like giant yellow squares in the green and rolling landscape.

Often, we could smell the crop's distinctive scent on the morning air as we walked through woods carpeted with wild flowers and along sunlit and shady lanes.

Further along the way, our hearts were set on a cool pint in the tiny hamlet of Hoar Cross, but surprise, surprise, it had closed, so we lunched in the porch of the 1870s-built Church of the Holy Angels, said by the late Sir John Betjeman to be the masterpiece of its Victorian architect, George Bodley.

An afternoon's walk brought us to our farmhouse B&B just outside Abbots Bromley, with its famous hexagonal Buttercross, and from there next morning we were soon crossing the Blithfield Reservoir causeway and on to again link up with the Trent and Mersey Canal.

Now followed a delightful morning's waterside walk to reach the 1850s-built Essex Bridge, the longest remaining packhorse bridge, in England, before moving on through the parklands of Shugborough Hall and climbing up on to wooded Cannock Chase.

Here we lost the way, but help was at hand when we came across a young man from Cannock, who was spending the day meditating beside his tent with his three terriers and pointed out the village of Brocton not far below us.

It was off the route, but was a landmark from which we could navigate our way back on course to our hotel stopover in Penkridge.

"Don't forget to stand on the Millennium sundial, which uses your body to create the shadow. You'll see it on your way down," the lad instructed, but as we reached it, the sun, which had been shining all day, suddenly went in!

Next morning, we set out along the Staffordshire and Worcestershire Canal, before walking on and stopping for coffee in picturesque Brewood.

Here we had to make a lengthy lane diversion to the market town of Shifnal, because all the accommodation near at hand was full, but were richly rewarded the following day when we rejoined with the way in the village of Beckbury.

We were now some miles into Shropshire and enjoyed a lovely day's cross-country walking to reach our journey's end in historic Ironbridge, where, somewhat to our dismay, we discovered the world's first iron bridge completely covered up as part of a £3,5 million restoration project.

"It's that Cosmic Joker up to his tricks again," said Peter as we tucked in to a celebration cream tea, while sitting outside a cafe just opposite in the afternoon sunshine.

But now we were experiencing yet another deja vu moment. For it was after a long day's walk on the Severn Way, some years previously, that we two tired walkers had stopped at a small café, further down the street, in the gathering gloom at closing time and the lady owner took pity on us

As a thank you, we presented her with a tea plate we'd found on the roadside earlier that afternoon.

Cross Britain Way – Part Four

We returned to Ironbridge for the next stage of our Cross Britain walk to find a most intriguing sight.

Five young women and one man were sitting around a table outside The Malt House pub, socialising in the evening sunshine - so what might be their connection?

"Maybe it's an office party," Peter suggested, as we sat inside by a window awaiting the arrival of our supper.

Ahead, lay eight glorious days of walking, first to Wenlock Edge, whose Olympian Games dating back to 1850 are a forerunner of the Olympics, and then on to attractive Church Stretton, before crossing the Shropshire Hills to descend into Wales, near Welshpool, and so beyond into the Snowdonia National Park

But first back to that intriguing little group.

As former journalists, our curiosity got the better of us, so Peter went out to discover that they were all teachers at the Coalbrookdale and Ironbridge Primary School celebrating the end of the summer term.

We had twenty miles to cover the following day, so we set off at 6am, stopping in a sunny field corner for orange juice, croissants, bananas and coffee.

By lunchtime, we'd walked all along the wooded Wenlock Edge escarpment and were entering the small village of Longville-in-the Dale, where there was a pub for a pint, but alas, as is so often the case, it had closed.

"You can join us for a drink if you like," invited a local, who was sitting in a nearby garden with his four sons and two friends, and had seen our plight.

Pint glasses of lemonade and a variety of crisps were quickly produced and we spent a happy hour eating our sandwiches and learning a little about their lives.

Spontaneous acts of kindness have often enriched our walking experience and others were in store further along the way.

We stayed overnight in Church Stretton, which has the air of an alpine resort about it, before setting out on a long, but scenic day's walk, over Shropshire's famous Long Mynd hills, followed by the Stiperstones plateaux, with its spectacular rock formations.

It was around 7pm when we walked wearily into the small village of Brocton, where the helpful landlady of The Cock Inn, had gone out of her way to find somewhere for us to stay and pub friends had volunteered their static caravan.

Two shorter days walking took us first over the border into Wales, where we were made most welcome at the comfortable Royal Oak in Welshpool, and then on to the small riverside village of Pont Robert, where we stayed overnight in a secluded 17th century farmhouse.

Now followed a delightful day's walk beside the River Vyrnwy along a series of wooded valleys to Llanwddyn at the end of Lake Vyrnwy.

En route at, Plas Dolanog, we got chatting to a sheep farmer and his wife, having walked through their yard, and she produced a jug of milk to top up our flasks.

"That's what you call the milk of human kindness," remarked Peter as they waved us on our way.

Peter had booked us in to a B&B in Llanwddyn and we soon found the house in row of properties on the hillside.

It was only 4pm and, not unsurprisingly, our hosts were not at home, so we opened a gate, wandered into their garden, made ourselves comfortable on a couple of seats and decided to finish up our coffee.

An hour later, they had still not returned and faint alarm bells began ringing, so Peter went and knocked on a neighbour's door only to discover that our hosts had recently moved and we had in fact been trespassing!

We had no mobile reception, but luckily there was an operational telephone box close by and our intended host, who had now moved to the other side of the valley, answered straight away and, full of apologies, said he would drive over and pick us up.

That evening he obligingly drove us to a smart hotel with magnificent views over Lake Vyrnwy, for an evening meal and home again afterwards.

This massive lake, we learned, was created when the valley was dammed to provide fresh water for the city of Liverpool, but there was a price to pay because the main village of Llanwddyn was submerged, only to reappear after a severe drought.

Following another overnight B&B, we spent a spectacular day walking, first beside Lake Vyrnwy, and then over the mountain on a remote single-track road to enter the Snowdonia National Park and drop down into the small and bustling tourist town of Bala.

From here the following morning, we walked down Lake Bala for a picnic breakfast on the flower-festooned Lake Bala Railway Station in Llanuwchllyn.

Here we met a couple on a volunteering holiday, busy preparing the steam engine, Maid Marion, for her daily service. They had previously lived in the area before moving up to Scotland, they told us.

A trek along a valley between high hills brought us into the small granite stone town of Dolgellau, now just nine miles from the end of our walk.

As we strolled along the scenic Mawddach Trail, a former railway line running beside a wide estuary, all the way to Barmouth, the following morning, we felt a sense of achievement, but also one of regret that another great adventure had finally reached the end of the road.

Guide book: Cross Britain Way - www.macmillanway.org/

CROSSING BRITAIN

In twenty days they crossed the land
From Boston Stump to Barmouth strand
From North Sea Wash to Irish Sea –
The years shrugged off past seventy
With book and maps they walked the ways
Through winter frosts and summer haze
Savouring each changing sight
Taking rests where'er they might
In flower-filled meadows, fields of corn -
At times a start 'fore break of dawn
With rucksacks packed for overnights
They crossed deep valleys, scaled the heights
Met with strangers, parted friends
Adventures waiting round each bend
Criss-crossing paths they'd strode before
Recalling times from memory's store

History present at each turn
Tales to gather, facts to learn
From Lincolnshire to Leicestershire
From wolds to forest dark
They headed West to Staffordshire
And bluebell-smothered park
Along canals and rivers
Then over Cannock Chase
The country miles unfolding
As they kept up their pace
They passed the gorge at Ironbridge –
The border drawing near
But first to scale the Stiperstones –
Their fractured crags so sheer
From Shropshire's hidden beauty
They entered mystic Wales
As high above the mountaintops
The soaring raptors sailed
The national park, Snowdonia
The perfect home run stage
Before they entered Barmouth
And turned the final page.

GOLDEN WEEDS

Along a bluebell-bordered lane
And through a metal gate
A meadow strewn with dandelions
Gold weeds in splendour wait
Shaded by a new-leafed tree
Quiet time to take their ease
Drowsing through the insect hum
And cooled by soft-blown breeze
A rest stop crossing Britain
On footpaths coast to coast
From Boston through to Barmouth
And that is no mean boast.

THE MOST UN-COMMON BLUE

Image: Pete Wilkins

A fragment of a perfect sky
Fluttering on the road
A vibrant flash of colour
The ancients knew as woad
Some other lepidoptera
Are blessed with pretty names
Like swallowtail and peacock
They wouldn't be the same
If they were known as common
Described just by their hue
Like this rare English beauty
The most un-common blue.

THE GRAND UNION & SHROPSHIRE UNION CANALS
Brentford to Chester – 200 miles

A laundry lady's kindness set us up for the day as we left the warmth of our motel room, slipped out into a foggy West London, morning and walked a few yards to a super highway of the19th century.

It was the start of a two-hundred-mile trek for Peter and I from London along the Grand Union Canal to Birmingham and on via the Shropshire Union Canal to historic Chester.

Disaster had struck earlier when our motel kettle failed to work, so there threatened to be no coffee for our rest stops.

Luckily, we bumped into a helpful member of staff, who deactivated the motel alarms, went into the kitchen and filled our flasks.

On reaching the 123-mile-long canal with its 166 locks on that cold and frosty morning, just before Christmas, we spotted a cast-iron marker telling us it was 82 miles to Braunston Junction, where the Grand Union meets the Oxford Canal and so on to Birmingham via lovely Leamington Spa.

Following a canal is like taking a fascinating walk into another world, suspended between the early 1800s, when the Grand Union was opened, and the hustle and bustle of today.

Quietly and largely unseen by thousands of motorists, who drive over its many bridges, it meanders its almost-subterranean way out of the capital and into the countryside.

'Don't spend so much time making a living that you forget to make a life,' advised the sign stuck to the window of one of the canal boats of all shapes, sizes and conditions we trudged past.

Sacks of coal, piles of logs, and even miniature gardens, covered their steel roofs as we passed, while bicycles padlocked to trees, a chicken coop complete with two large Rhode Island Reds and even a wardrobe graced the towpath along the way.

'Need to Home Educate Your Children?' asked the note in another window, while a third sought converts to a canal-side ministry by advertising a towpath service.

It was dusk when we climbed steps to emerge, Tardis-like, into busy Hunton Bridge, where we were staying for the night.

Early the following morning and back on the canal beside a main railway line, the thumpity-thump of commuter trains grabbed our attention as their illuminated carriages flashed by causing vivid reflections in the dark waters beside us.

Soon we were received Hobbit-like within the towering concrete portals of the mighty M25 as it spanned the canal, looking in the gloom like some vast cathedral.

Saying farewell to the motorway was like shaking ourselves free of the metropolis, knowing that mostly green and pleasant lands lay ahead.

Now it was time for breakfast in Hemel Hempstead, where architects have made the most of the canal by creating a complex of homes surrounding a marina.

We ate in a coffee shop and were soon following the canal as it began its lock-by-lock ascent into the wooded hills and forward to picturesque Berkhamsted.

Here, as in many other cases, the canal passes through the heart of the busy market town en route to Tring and the highest point of the Grand Union on its way through the Chilterns.

We descended into the Vale of Aylesbury, on to Leighton Buzzard, forward to Milton Keynes and so at last to Braunston, where there was time for a browse in the Canal and River Trust shop.

It's a lovely day's walk from there into Leamington Spa and a further two days to Birmingham and its famous Gas Street Basin, a major hub of the UK's waterways system with its waterfront bars and restaurants.

Despite the urban sprawl between here and Wolverhampton, the fifteen miles are surprisingly leafy and once through this conurbation, Thomas Telford's magnificent Shropshire Union Canal awaits.

Now followed six days of lovely rural and sometimes surprisingly remote walking through Staffordshire and Cheshire, with overnight stopovers in Market Drayton, Nantwich and Tarporley and so on to historic Chester.

Beyond Norbury Junction in a gloomy cutting we encountered Bridge 39, said to be haunted by a black monkey-like creature.

"Come out wherever you are," Peter called out, but no sooner were the words out of his mouth, then he stumbled on a loose stone and almost fell flat on his face.

We completed the walk in sections and it was on returning to Market Drayton to recommence with a night's stay at the Four Alls Inn that we encountered our second act of kindness.

I was shocked to discover that chilly March evening that I had left my fleece at home, but help was at hand thanks to our landlady publican, who luckily had a spare one.

The following day when the canal narrowed to pass under a bridge, we hailed a passing boat steered by an ambulance driver from Shrewsbury, who happily gave us the experience of a lift to the next lock.

That afternoon as we approached Tarporley, we came across a retired farrier and his wife from Mountain Ash in South Wales, who had lived on the canals for some years and loved their life.

He had turned half a metal beer barrel into a forge and was making hinges and horseshoes, which his wife painted. He also gathered ash and beech along the way and made stools and magnificent walking sticks.

The couple had two narrowboats, on top of one of which lived their two ferrets, Nip and Tuck, which they used to catch rabbits - later to be turned into Bunny Burgers for visiting grandchildren.

From Tarporley, which is two miles off the canal, it was an easy day's walk into Chester, where we celebrated with a stay at the magnificent Queen Hotel, said to be the oldest railway hotel in the world.

Guide books: Cicerone Guides' Grand Union Canal Walk, London to Birmingham - www.cicerone.co.uk/ and J,M. Pearson's Canal Companion: Welsh Waters - www.jmpearson.co.uk/

A CANAL LABELLED GRAND

Before the steam-powered Rocket
Came chugging down the line
And well before that HS2
Would ill-thought schemes define
Canals were super highways
So that's why it was planned
To London link with Birmingham
A union labelled Grand
From Brentford in the capital
And up to Milton Keynes
Grubby suburbs giving way
To pleasant rural scenes
At Braunston there's a junction
Where water-dwellers meet
The walkers passed by briskly
Conveyed on booted feet
To reach the Gas Street Basin's
Hubbub with noisy bars
Before they took the towpath North
To leave the world of cars

The Shropshire Union peaceful
And there they chanced to meet
A couple with two ferrets
Their life afloat complete
Finale then in Chester,
Where Romans strode the walls,
Knowing they could not resist
More towpaths' siren calls.

THE HEART OF ENGLAND WAY
Cannock Chase to Bourton-on-the-Water – 102 miles

It was quite a tough first morning on the Heart of England Way for Peter and I – climbing steeply and then descending equally sharply, along woodland tracks and through open heathland on Cannock Chase in Staffordshire.

Despite having a detailed guide book and the appropriate OS maps, we still managed to miss our path having spent little more than an hour on this wonderful 102-mile trail.

But luckily, help was at hand with the sudden appearance of two local dog walkers, who put us back on the right track beside the moving Katyn Memorial.

This commemorates the 14,000 Polish officers and others, who were brutally murdered by the Russians in the Katyn Forest, near Smolensk in 1940, and it was erected after a fund-raising campaign by a local Polish man, who saw a similarity between the two wooded locations.

We picnicked just below the Castle Ring, an Iron Age hill fort high up on the southern edge of Cannock Chase, and with five miles still to go to that day's journeys end in Lichfield, we decided to leave the trail and walk along quiet sunlit lanes instead.

This allowed us to stop and rest our weary legs with a refreshing pint in the coolness of The Malt Shovel in the pretty flower-decked village of Chorley.

Alas, the magnificent façade of Lichfield Cathedral was in deep shadow and not worth a picture, so venturing inside, we spent thirty memorable minutes listening to choristers rehearsing for Evensong.

Emerging into the bright early evening sunshine, we found the cathedral bathed in light and got our picture after all.

After a comfortable night's stay with dinner at the nearby George Hotel, we were poised to depart when I spotted an ant crawling around the wash basin! He'd clearly climbed aboard my person, when I had accidentally put my map case down on his nest the previous afternoon.

Feeling somewhat responsible for this tiny fellow traveller, I scooped it up in a tissue and sent it parachuting down to freedom through the open bedroom window.

Finding our way back to a trail from the busy centres of towns and cities has often posed a problem and with Lichfield being no exception, I wondered how my ant was getting along!

An hour later, we were finally walking away from the city and onward for mile after mile across a flat landscape, amid fields of golden crops, under leaden skies.

Then, bearing right on a long curve of dusty farm tracks, we came upon the first of several nasty scars being made by contractors working on the route of HS2, and leaving it behind, we crossed the busy A5 and headed up into the rolling hills ahead.

Descending again, we made our way across country, passing more HS2 workings, to reach the village of Drayton Bassett, where we picnicked in the churchyard.

From there it was a short step to the Birmingham and Fazeley Canal, where we crossed the famous folly-like footbridge, built in 1830 at the same time as the since-demolished Dayton Manor, former home of Sir Robert Peel, who later became Prime Minister.

Now the sun came out and we followed this quiet waterway for several miles to our overnight stop at The Marston Farm Hotel.

En route, we passed Warwickshire County Council's Kingsbury Water Park, comprising fifteen lakes and created by gravel extraction to provide a 600-acre haven for wildlife, anglers, water sports enthusiasts and fellow walkers.

It was now Day Three on our walk, across open and undulating country, amid more ripening cereal crops and through shady woodland and quiet villages to come at last to our overnight stop in Meriden.

Here a surprise was in store because neither Peter nor I had ever come across a war memorial dedicated to cyclists.

Yet every year, cyclists from all over the country, descend on this Warwickshire village, which claims to be the historic heart of England - hence the name of our walk - to honour those brave cyclists, who had fallen in combat during two World Wars.

We left our Strawberry Bank Hotel, where we had enjoyed an excellent supper, at 7.15am for our final day walking some 17 miles across country to picturesque Henley-in-Arden.

An early close encounter for a third time with the line of HS2, not far beyond the pretty village of Berkswell with its lovely Saxon Church of St John Baptist, caused a diversion and delay as monster earth-moving trucks went trundling past.

From then on, the path wound its way through crop fields and hay meadows to eventually reach the Grand Union Canal, which we followed to its junction with the Stratford Canal and then along this waterway almost as far as the small village of Lowsonford.

Here we left the canal for a late afternoon walk over the hills to ascend a grassy knoll for a magnificent finale view over Henley-in-Arden and the surrounding wooded countryside.

Dropping down a steeply-sloping path into the village, we passed several empty seats and I remarked how strange it was that no one appeared to be around to appreciate the view on such a lovely afternoon.

Then, as if right on cue, a young couple appeared strolling hand-in-hand towards us, with their whole young lives ahead of them!

The Heart of England Way – Part Two

Peter and I have been trekking the highways and byways of Britain for 40-odd years staying in hotels, inns and B&Bs along the way, but never before had we been served our breakfast coffee in a teapot!

It happened when we returned to The White Swan, a popular and comfortable coaching inn in picturesque Henley-in-Arden to complete the second part of the Heart of England Way.

This historic inn is more or less midway between the start of this 102-mile walk from Cannock Chase in Staffordshire, through Warwickshire, to Bourton-on-the-Water in Gloucestershire.

The teapot kept our coffee hot and the brew was easy to pour, so variety was the spice of life, we agreed.

We set off early on an October morning with the sun just rising behind us and were quickly out into open country with the way leading across farmland and over wooded hillsides tinged with the gold of Autumn.

We picnicked on the edge of a large plantation and did not meet a single soul until entering the pretty market town of Alcester in the early afternoon.

I wanted to take a picture, but annoyingly the sun started playing hide and seek with me.

Spotting a small teashop, we bought chocolate brownies for later, but they came in two cake boxes, which were not backpack friendly!

Finding our way out of town proved more difficult than entering it, because we missed a turning, but were soon trudging up a winding path and contouring around the hilltop site of Oversley Castle with fabulous views across to a line of distant hills, which I assumed to be the Cotswolds.

It was the perfect spot to stop and polish off those brownies.

Descending the hill in the late afternoon, we came upon the hamlet of Wixford and the Three Horseshoes, which looked to be closed, but a face appeared in the window and we were beckoned inside for a welcome pint.

I ordered some prawn crackers, but they came not in a packet as expected, but in a large bowl with a chilli dip. "Don't worry, what we don't eat now can go in one of those cake boxes for later," said Peter.

It was now just a couple of miles to our homely B&B in the High Street in Bidford-on-Avon and as the light was fading, we decided to leave the path and take the road into Bidford, which is also a staging post on the Shakespeare's Avon Way.

Crossing the village's ancient arched bridge, spanning the Avon, early the following morning, we began the next fourteen-mile section of the walk to Chipping Campden in the now not so faraway Cotswolds.

A fine drizzle cleared as we reached higher ground, under big unsettled skies, and a green Heart of England Way sign showed us taking the higher of two grassy paths over a hill.

But then it seemed to be curving back on itself, the signs had disappeared and a study of our OS map indicated that we had wandered off course.

"What we need now is a local dog walker," Peter declared and as he did so, a Springer Spaniel came scampering around the corner.

His owner directed us to a lane leading into the delightful hamlet of Dorsington, which was back on our route, and we stopped for a coffee, while admiring a cluster of old red brick houses, all with thatched roofs.

Now we walked to Long Marston and then on a long loop through farmland to reach the villages of Lower and Upper Quinton.

Beyond the villages, the way began another long loop around wooded Meon Hill and forward to the village of Mickleton.

Stopping en route to admire the view and munch our sandwiches, I eagerly opened my box of prawn crackers, but of course by now they'd lost all their crunch!

Strangely, it's not often that we meet kindred spirits, who walk as we do on a regular basis, but then we came across four women walkers from Nottingham taking a break outside St Lawrence Parish Church.

Leaving Mickleton, the way now led up a steep hill and followed a long and often wooded hillside before dropping down into Chipping Campden, which has arguably one of the finest High Streets in England.

We celebrated with toasted teacakes in a café before walking the final few yards to the comfortable Noel Arms, a sixteenth century coaching hotel, where we were booked in for dinner and the night.

The weather took a turn for the worse the following morning and we walked out of Chipping Campden in the pouring rain and made our way to the smaller, but equally picturesque village of Broad Campden.

From here the way led over the hills and down into Blockley, yet another Cotswold gem, and on via Longborough to the oddly-named Upper and Lower Swell and finally to Lower Slaughter where the sun at last broke free of the clouds in the late afternoon.

Now we were just a couple of miles from yet another journey's end in the iconic Cotswold town of Bourton-on-the Water and the sun shone all the way.

Guide book: The Heart of England Way Association's guide book by Stephen Cross - www.heartofenglandway.org As the HS2 was being rolled out across the landscape when we were out on the trail, route alterations may well be worth checking.

CATHEDRAL CHORUS

Beneath three spires a-soaring
Within the walls so strong
The sound of voices rising
Before the evensong
Gathered choirs rehearsing
Conductor keeping time
Organ music background
For moment so sublime
Outside in brilliant sunshine
Cathedral bathed in light
Jewel of fair Lichfield
As bells make birds take flight.

HS2 VIEW

HS2, HS2
What on earth's the point of you
Carving up the countryside
Homes and farms are smashed aside
All to save just half an hour
For those who live in ivory tower
The billions spent on this fool scheme
More politicians' sad pipe dream.

SPINDLEBERRY DAY

A burnished English hedgerow
In early morning light
Henley set in Arden
Now finally out of sight
Summer's fallen finery
Strewn along the way
Of winding paths through woodland
On sun-blessed autumn day
Scattered leaf profusion
In shades of brown and yellow
Beneath the trees that overhang
Half-hidden track to follow
Cascades of spindleberries
Round shady corner found
Lead to where crab apples
Lie carpeting the ground.

PUMPKIN SPREE

A field of orange pumpkins
As Halloween draws near
Children running gaily
Each tended row to clear
Their prizes stacked in barrow
And then back home to race
Where underneath a skilful knife
Appears a scary face.

THE HUDDERSFIELD NARROW CANAL
Huddersfield to Ashton-under-Lyne – 20 miles

Oh, how perverse life can be at times, I thought as Peter and I looked out over the Huddersfield Narrow Canal basin while having an early breakfast in a most conveniently-situated Premier Inn.

We were about to set out on the walk of around 20 miles along this delightful waterway, which once served huge former red brick woollen mills with towering chimneys and other poignant reminders of Britain's world-leading industrial revolution.

But 'No', just stepping outside was not going to be possible because there was a tunnel a couple of hundred yards away without an accompanying towpath.

This would now mean a detour through busy city streets until, hopefully, we came across a convenient access point.

It would not be the first time we'd got lost trying to find a canal in the midst of a metropolis, but luckily help was at hand on this occasion when we soon spotted a blue cycle route and towpath sign.

The Huddersfield Narrow Canal, straddling the Pennines, which took thousands of pick and shovel-wielding labourers seventeen long years to build and opened in 1811, winds its way amid rugged hills and through wooded countryside along the Colne river valley.

It has two unique claims to fame in that at 645 feet above sea level it is the highest in Britain, while its Standedge Tunnel, being over three miles in length, is the longest, deepest and, of course, highest in the land.

It took twenty-seven years of campaigning and restoration by the Huddersfield Canal Society before this magnificent waterway was fully reopened to navigation back in 2001 and became one of only three Pennine crossings, the others being the Rochdale and the Leeds and Liverpool canals.

As winter is a busy season for maintenance, with few narrowboats on the water, we came upon three separate teams working on behalf of Britain's Canal and River Trust, busy cutting back trees, repairing a lock paddle and even shoring up a bank by injecting a special compound.

Approaching flask of coffee time and on reaching a lock, we came upon the former Titanic woollen mill, so named by locals because it was built in 1911 – the year that the ill-fated liner was launched.

Like many other industrial edifices, it has been given a new lease of life by being converted into apartments, but back in its heyday it held the world record for producing a suit from wool to wearer in just two hours and ten minutes!

Not long after, the canal ran right through the heart of the picturesque and bustling west Yorkshire village of Linthwaite, where we were almost enticed into a waterfront café for another coffee and perhaps a piece of cake.

That's the beauty of canal walking - you never know quite what sights you are going to come upon just around the next bend.

By lunch time we'd ascended 45 locks to the canal's highest point in the village of Marsden and spent a comfortable hour in the busy Riverhead Brewery Tap, listening to snatches of conversation from the locals and enjoying lunch in the warm.

It was William Horsfall. owner of Ottiwells Mill in Marsden, who was set upon and murdered by three Luddites, afraid that their traditional weaving skills would be swept away by the ceaseless advance of mechanisation.

We were now close to the Standedge Tunnel, but being winter, there were no boats on which to hitch a ride and, as it was going to be getting dark in a couple of hours, there was no time to follow a path over the top, so we called a local taxi.

A short and misty ride over the Pennines brought us to our overnight pub stop close to the canal in the curiously-named village of Diggle, which is apparently derived from the Saxon name 'Deggle' meaning Valley.

We were back on the canal early in the morning for our ten-mile walk to journey's end near the busy towns of Stalybridge and Ashton-under-Lyne, where this waterway links up with the Ashton Canal to Manchester and the Peak Forest Canal towards Macclesfield.

Now the locks were descending into the Tame Valley, close to the River Tame, which began life as the Diggle Brook, high in the hills above the village.

It was not long before we came upon the welcoming Lime Kiln Café, close to a magnificent Victorian railway viaduct, carrying the Manchester line.

Now followed an interesting morning's walk along the Tame Valley through the villages of Upper Mill, Greenfield and Mossley with glimpses of gradually-descending Pennine ridges on either side.

We might have missed the mighty Standedge Tunnel, which takes two hours to cruise through, but a small treat was now in store.

For we suddenly found ourselves approaching the 200-yard-long Scout Tunnel with, luckily, a walkway and handrail all the way through and so made a fitting finale to our latest canal adventure.

Guide book: J.M Pearson's Canal Companion: Cheshire Ring and South Pennine Ring - www.jmpearson.co.uk/

PENNINES DIVIDED

Ghost mills that once wove cotton
Disused like mills of wool
The high Pennines dividing
Where industry did rule
The rushing Colne alongside
Canal in stone banks tamed
Past monumental building
For lost Titanic named
Long gone the busy workers
Who once world record made
Fleece to wearer in two hours
A fine suit then displayed.
From Huddersfield to Marsden
Where mournful church bells rang
When Luddites fighting progress
Were taken out to hang
Beyond, the Standedge Tunnel
The longest and most high
And deepest in the country
But closed, so we passed by.

TUNNEL VISION

Canal Scout Tunnel vision
Emerging to the light
After yards of cobbled path
Where day was turned to night
Like a mini Standedge
Blasted through the hill
Lined with brick at start and end
But bedrock showing still
A rail to guard the walkers
Lest they should take a fall
Head torch on to pierce the gloom
Beside the damp-run wall
The ghosts of bygone boatmen
Accompany each pace
Along this water highway
Within this Pennine place.

LEEDS AND LIVERPOOL CANAL
Liverpool to Leeds – 127 miles

Many memorable journeys have started from Britain's great ports and none more so than from Liverpool on the banks of the mighty river Mersey.

From here in times past countless souls have sailed forth seeking new lives over the rainbow of their dreams and even today ferries sail to Ireland and cruise ships depart for sunnier climes.

Peter and I were also starting out on a long journey, but we were turning our backs on the Mersey and following the 127-mile-long canal from Liverpool to Leeds.

We'd travelled up by train from Bristol and after a night spent appropriately in an old Albert Dock warehouse, superbly transformed into a comfortable Premier Inn, we set out walking along the promenade beside the river heading for the old Stanley Dock and the Stanley flight of locks, accessing the canal.

We were soon dwarfed by what is believed to be the world's largest brick-built warehouse, where President Roosevelt's wife, Eleanor, visited wounded GIs towards the end of World War Two

Here we met a Canal and River Trust volunteer lock-keeper waiting to lock in the first of the hundreds of narrowboats and other craft we were to see along the way.

He told us how German warplanes used to strafe the canal to disrupt its floating traffic and how bullet holes, as we were later to confirm, could still be seen in the stone bridge parapets nearby.

Further on we came across fellow volunteers busy pulling a supermarket trolley out of the water as part of a regular rubbish-collecting and litter-picking exercise.

Having put some miles behind us, we picnicked beside the canal close to the Primrose Valley Country Park and then walked on towards Aintree, the home of the famous racecourse, where we were conveniently booked into another Premier Inn, this one, the Liverpool North, just a couple of minutes' walk from the canal.

En route, we stopped for at least five minutes to watch as two male coots ferociously battled it out beak and claw for the intentions of a female, who seemed to have already made her choice, as she kept darting in and pecking the outsider until he was eventually driven off.

We were on our way again just as the sun was rising over the water ahead of us and casting an orange autumnal glow that made me blink and we knew we would still be walking when it started to dip towards the West in late afternoon.

For it was some sixteen miles trek to journey's end in the West Lancashire village of Burscough, where Peter had booked us into an hotel conveniently close to the canal.

"Have you got your head torch handy?" I asked Peter, only to hear that it was buried somewhere in the bottom of his rucksack.

Walking across the country on a long-distance trail, always moving on and never going back, is like savouring a cross-section of town and rural life and so it was on that Saturday morning when we entered the small town of Maghull to meet a merry party of sixteen-year-olds out on a sponsored canal walk for the Alzheimer's Society.

Then further on along the embankment, we were looking down on the local playing fields, where a number of football games, involving groups of young people, were in full swing.

It wasn't until around midday that we finally walked out into open country and felt that Liverpool and its environs were well and truly behind us.

While squadrons of ducks cruised in and out of the reeds and the occasional skein of Canada geese flew in V formations across the pale blue skies, we walked ever on through patches of beech woodland, golden in the weak afternoon sun and past dense fields of leeks and other winter crops.

It was around 4.30pm and on approaching Burscough that we met a lady dog walker and asked how far it was to our hotel.

"Oh! that's miles away," came her shock reply – our chosen hotel it turned out was not on the main canal, but on its Rufford Arm.

She said we should walk on past the village for about a mile, until we came to this subsidiary of the canal and then should turn down that until we'd eventually come to the hotel, she instructed.

Our pace had slackened in anticipation of journey's end, but now we picked it up again with some urgency as the deployment of our head torches was suddenly a real possibility.

We reached the Rufford Arm turning in a twenty-minute march only to discover from another local that the hotel was another hour's walk away along this arm and therefore impossible to reach in daylight.

And when we discovered that a section of the towpath was closed for repairs, we gave up the attempt and luckily found a local taxi driver to pick us up shortly and take us to the hotel.

This was a completely understandable mistake because when Peter booked the hotel, said to be only a few yards from the canal, he had no idea that the canal had a separate arm!

Sadly, it was now time to leave the canal at the end of the first stage of our walk and the following morning, a taxi took us back to Liverpool to catch our train back to Bristol.

But it happened to be Armistice Sunday and we were dropped by the city's Cenotaph, as a huge crowd bowed their heads in a respectful silence as a lone bugler played The Last Post.

Then thousands of paper poppies began floating down on the cold and frosty morning air and Peter was inspired to complete a poem he had started a year before about those released at the annual Festival of Remembrance in the Royal Albert Hall – **see Scarlet Rain – Page 84.**

We returned after Christmas and spent the night in a B&B close this time to the main canal before heading back to the towpath.

The official responsible for measuring the Leeds and Liverpool canal, Britain's longest single man-made waterway, which took over forty years to build and opened back in 1816, must have been obsessed with exactitude.

For according to him or her, it was exactly 127 and a quarter miles long!

Why on Earth, they didn't lose that pesky quarter rather than having to include it on every single mile post along the entire route we simply couldn't imagine.

Still, it provided an amusing topic of conversation for Peter and I as we set out on the second stage of our journey.

A 90-minute walk brought us to the small West Lancashire village of Parbold, beyond which we entered the Douglas Valley in company with the meandering River Douglas and followed it to pass under the M6 high on a massive flyover.

What a contrast, a super highway of the 19th century meeting that of the 21st.

Walking into Wigan, we passed the Wigan Pier cultural quarter, opened by the Queen in 1986, and the massive Eckersley Mill complex nearby, now a site of dereliction, and learned that the area had made a perfect setting for the hit TV drama, Peaky Blinders!

A magnificent flight of locks on the edge of Wigan led the way quickly out of this busy town the following morning at the beginning of our ten-mile walk to Chorley.

We'd not gone far before we came upon two pensioners, sitting on a bridge wall and chatting in the sunshine.

The women turned out to be kindred spirits in that they completed a three-mile circuit, including the canal, every morning to keep themselves fit and really missed the exercise if something prevented them from doing so.

Soon the long line of the West Pennine moors hove into view - an exciting prospect of more lovely scenery to come.

That afternoon, we were surprised to come across a red double-decker bus and delighted to find that it had been converted into a canal-side tea shop, so we climbed aboard for welcome mugs of tea and a Bakewell tart.

We overnighted in Chorley and had only been back on the canal for about forty minutes when, to our surprise and dismay the waterway came to a dead end in a jumble of reeds, completely impeding any possible narrowboat navigation.

Where on earth had we gone wrong?

But thankfully help was at hand when our knock on the door of a nearby house in Whittle-le-Woods was answered by a lady called Louise, who explained that we'd simply walked right past a side lock further back along the canal.

"Oh! dozens of people make the same mistake and on summer weekends we can have as many as twenty very confused walkers and cyclists all going around in circles before knocking on our door and asking for directions," she said.

Luckily, all we had to do was to walk up the road to the next bridge to re-join the canal.

Now we were back in some lovely open country with a hill rising on one side and a valley below us on the other.

Those distinctive white and black-lettered mile-and-a-quarter markers were our constant companions and we actually came across one which been half-swallowed by a tree!

"How far have you walked?" asked a lad in a peaked cap as we trudged wearily into Blackburn.

"From Chorley," I replied. "Cor, I wear my shoes out just walking to the job centre," he replied.

We passed several large red brick reminders of Blackburn's industrial past, including one formerly used as Granada TV studios, as we walked out of the city early the following morning.

We were on a bit of a mission because we needed to walk the sixteen miles into Burnley before we lost the late afternoon light.

Around midday we came upon the 200-year-old ruins of coke ovens at the former Aspen Colliery in Church, known locally as the Fairy Caves, and from there it was a short step to the official half-way point on the Leeds and Liverpool Canal.

The views now opened up as the canal contoured around the rising landscape in a series of wide curves, until at last we met the M65, which accompanied us to journey's end in the Lancashire town of Burnley.

From here to the small hillside town of Barnoldswick in West Yorkshire, the canal has a unique claim to fame,

For it is hard-surfaced for the whole of its meandering 14-mile route - first through a semi-urban environment and then out into magnificent open country with views of the Western Pennines.

This is an absolute gift for those hardy souls more used to sloshing along grassy and muddy paths.

We next reached a tunnel, where there was no towpath, and while boaters enjoy the subterranean experience of passing through, finding a way over the top can be more challenging for those on foot, but luckily a helpful dog walker came along to point out a country lane route.

Back in 1912, a cow called Buttercup fell into the canal at the western end of the tunnel and swam all the way through, before being rescued and revived with brandy.

Beyond the tunnel, we came across the welcoming Cafe Cargo converted from the stone-built headquarters of a local haulage company in the days of the horse and cart.

Now followed a delightful three-mile walk into the hillside town of Barnoldswick, where we stayed overnight before setting out for the picturesque Yorkshire Dales tourist centre of Skipton some fourteen miles ahead.

This was a blustery day of showers and strong winds, courtesy of a storm called Gareth, although there were sunny spells with more magnificent Pennine views as we joined the Pennine Way for a while before moving forward from Lancashire into West Yorkshire.

We trudged into the famous tourist honeypot of Skipton, the gateway to the Dales, at around four in the afternoon.

I say trudged because the stormy weather had taken its toll, buffeting us as we walked along a particularly exposed east-facing section of the bank before, thankfully turning north again for the final mile or two into this delightful, centuries-old market town.

Finding a cosy tea shop where we could take off our heavy packs and rest awhile was now our top priority and luckily we did not have too far to go to find one perched high above the canal.

As it was now late afternoon, the customer peak had subsided, which was good news, because we tend to become the centre of attention while divesting ourselves of our sacks and map cases and finding somewhere to park our walking poles without them sliding to the floor with a clatter.

Skipton, a small and friendly town with cobbled side streets, originally grew as a wealthy sheep and wool trading centre and is dominated by its magnificent castle, parish church and traditional high street market place.

Now revived, we set off on a three-mile stroll along the canal to our destination for the night, and were joined by a young man and his dog.

He was on his way to a nearby village to spend the evening watching sport on the telly with a friend before walking home again.

We returned to the canal in the Spring and stayed in a charming three-storey Victorian house in the village of Cononley before re-joining the canal as it contoured around a wide valley close to the River Aire.

A short walk brought us to the small town of Silsden with its cluster of old textile mills, now like many others along the route converted into apartments, so we climbed the steps beside the bridge to find a coffee shop.

The canal now wound its way around a narrow valley, where kingfishers skimmed its quiet waters, before we reached Riddlesden, where we stopped for a bowl of warming soup in The Marquis of Granby who, Google told us, had been a 16th Century general and national hero.

A short afternoon stroll found us at the top of the spectacular Five Locks Rise on the outskirts of Bingley and close to our overnight hotel stop.

Standing on top of this truly impressive flight, early the following morning, I studied our OS map to take a closer look at the route for our final 16-mile walk to journey's end.

Canal art en route

It skirted the Bradford conurbation, winding its way into the very heart of the city and looked heavily built-up and most unattractive, but what a surprise was in store.

For there were long stretches of woodland and open country along a narrow corridor, joined on occasion by the nearby River Aire.

We passed Saltaire, where philanthropist Sir Titus Salt built a textile mill and village for his valued workers and then on to Apperley Bridge, where we called at the Canal and River Trust office and met a towpath fund-raiser.

She showed us a framed document, which was a bill of sale for goods carried on the canal over 100 years ago.

The Railway Inn at Calverley Bridge made a most welcome lunch stop with just six miles of our ten-day, 127-mile journey still to go and was followed by an afternoon cuppa at the tiny canal-side café run by the Hollybush Environmental Volunteering Centre.

This charity has been operating for over 40 years and maintains threatened green spaces around Leeds and beyond.

True to recent form, and as I had spotted on our trusty OS map earlier, the canal surprisingly remained a largely green lung right into the heart of Leeds, where we were suddenly overwhelmed by bars, cafes and restaurants and hundreds of late Friday afternoon revellers.

What a sharp contrast to the miles and miles of open country we had walked through to get there.

The words from a famous hit pop song came floating into my head, as feeling quite disorientated, we went in search of our hotel for the night...'We gotta to get out of this place if it's the last thing we ever do!"

Guide book: J.M Pearson's Canal Companion: Leeds and Liverpool - www.jmpearson.co.uk/

WALKING THE CANAL

From Lancashire to Yorkshire
From Liverpool to Leeds
Canals dug deep by navvies
To meet commercial needs
Cutting through the landscape
From moors to sweeping dale
Linking Northern cities
'Fore losing place to rail
Towpaths that once knew hoofprints
Now marked by walkers' boots
Gone the hardy watermen
Who toiled upon these routes
Clear markers by the wayside
Counting down the miles
When joggers met along the track
A switch to single file
Kingfisher flash so fleeting
White stately swans serene
Leaning trees reflected
Upon the limpid green
Factory grime, satanic mills
Interchanged with rural charm
Slender bridges linking
Bisected fields on lonely farm

Lock gates that once awaited
Those urgent cargoes past
Now just closed and opened
For lazy pleasure craft
Rich heritage of industry
Surviving 'til today
Canal network of Britain
Still with a part to play.

DRY REQUISITE TROUSERS

Trousers known as plastic
Were once essential gear
For walkers when they set out
And rain clouds did appear
But they were really awkward
To put on in a rush
Dancing round on one leg
As footpaths turned mush
No sooner were they fitted
Then back would come the sun
And out from them you'd struggle
They really were no fun
Now Rohan have the trousers
That make a perfect fit
In shower or heavy downpour
They're called Dry Requisite
They look good when you're walking
But smart enough for town
You have a choice of colours
Some go for grey or brown
So now though storms may threaten
You need to have no fear
With legs not damp but cosy
In Rohan's first class gear.

SCARLET RAIN

Through the air like souls descending
Softly falls the scarlet rain
Blood red petals without number
Shower the living who remain
Echoes of those far-off poppies
Blooming where so many died
Scythed to earth – a bitter harvest
Legacy of power and pride
Sons and fathers, friends and strangers
Marching on, they fought and fell
Now beneath a white cross forest
Side by side forever dwell
Valiant soldiers still remembered
In each corner of the land
Those who owe a debt so heavy
Bowed in silent tribute stand.
In towns and cities 'cross the nations
Again is heard the bugle's call
Guns boom out to signal silence
Saluting those in death's cold thrall
Time to pause and just remember
The brave, the fearful, all as one
Never more to laugh with comrades
Never more to feel the sun
Those who marched out hale and hopeful
Are numbered now among the slain
But not unsung, nor yet forgotten
As softly falls the scarlet rain.

THE LLANGOLLEN CANAL
Hurleston Junction to Llangollen – 46 miles

It was early Spring when Peter and I set out on the picturesque Llangollen Canal.

This famous waterway, opened in 1805, links Llangollen in North Wales with Hurleston in South Cheshire and had been on our to-do list, ever since we passed its junction while walking the Shropshire Union Canal.

The Llangollen Canal was built during the industrial revolution, mainly to transport coal from South Denbighshire and to link with the wider canal network via the rivers Mersey, Dee and Severn.

A sulking sun suddenly burst through the clouds early on that dull April morning and all at once the hedgerows were ablaze with a confetti of white blossom, while the wood anemones, primroses and cyclamen scattered along the towpath shone with a brighter hue.

We were now en route for the small Northern market town of Whitchurch, some fourteen miles ahead, across a dead flat landscape with the first hints of yellow oil seed rape crops visible in surrounding fields.

Every now and again a narrowboat puttered by with an exchange of friendly waves.

"Just walk for another forty minutes and then cross the lift bridge to reach the town," instructed a helpful lady in the chanced-upon canalside café, where we had stopped for tea and cake.

We reached the bridge to find a fingerpost with the single word 'town' pointing along a small connecting waterway and our hopes rose that after eight hours on the path, journey's end was at last in sight.

But sadly, it was not to be, because the towpath eventually petered out in a small housing estate and we were then led, siren-like, along a series of linking footpaths to emerge onto a road.

"Just walk up through the park and you'll be in the town," we were relieved to hear from a passer-by.

After a hearty meal in the friendly Bulls Head and a good night's rest in our B&B, our previously flagging spirits revived and we were back on the trail again, although the weather had taken a turn for the worse.

Soon we came across a West Country couple, who had acquired their boat the previous summer and now planned to spend their future cruising around the country.

Then the rain set in and the towpath, quite uneven in places, soon became slippery and our trusty walking poles came into their own.

Again, our way led through remote open country with only one small village between us and journey's end in the small market town of Ellesmere, another twelve miles ahead.

Now we entered a large fenland area and nature reserve with small lakes created by old peat diggings and the sounds of wildfowl were soon filling the air.

The waterway was wider here and dead straight for several miles, so it was simply a case of putting our hooded heads down and trudging onward.

But then the rain stopped and the canal began meandering across a higher and more wooded landscape and here we came upon a cheery team of Canal and River Trust engineers.

They were busy shoring up a collapsing section of bank, a massive on-going operation when one considers the whole of the waterways network.

Walking on under clearer, yet misty skies, we were now enjoying views over two large lakes, which according to our OS map were called 'Meres,' hence Ellesmere, we concluded.

Like Whitchurch, this turned out to be a small market town with winding streets and a host of old buildings.

Back on the towpath early the following morning, we soon came upon the junction with the Montgomery Canal, linking with Welshpool and Newtown in Mid-Wales, and another future walk just added itself to our list.

Later, the canal began meandering through rolling folds in the landscape with now, not so distant, Welsh hills encircling the sunny rural scene and a series of locks, not encountered for many a mile, began lifting the canal gently onto higher ground.

Not far ahead, we came upon the impressive 70-foot-high and 710-foot-long cast-iron Chirk Aqueduct, built on stone piers by engineers Thomas Telford and William Jessop to carry the canal across the Ceiriog Valley.

A nose-to-tail flotilla of narrowboats came towards us, some of which we guessed had over-wintered further up the canal and were now migrating to spend the rest of the summer months roaming across the country.

Another treat was in store ahead when we walked through the 460-yard-long Chirk Tunnel guided by a hand rail and a distant dot of light.

Beyond the tunnel, a convenient footpath led us up to a road and into the small town of Chirk and so to that day's journey's end and our overnight hotel stopover.

We were back on the towpath by 8am for what promised to be the most scenic and interesting final nine miles of the walk.

A carpet of wood anemones cascaded down through woodland as we approached the much shorter Whitehouse Tunnel and then on to a famous highlight of the walk, namely Telford and Jessop's dramatic Pontcysyllte Aqueduct.

This spectacular 336-yard-long, 126-foot-high and 18-arch stone and cast-iron triumph of industrial architecture, carries the canal across the River Dee in the Vale of Llangollen

Soon we were contouring around a wide valley amid high hills with the town of Llangollen and the River Dee far below us, en route for journey's end at the Horseshoe Falls.

But first we had to step aside for a horse-drawn narrowboat packed with tourists. a sight that would have left any time-travelling and hardy yesteryear boatman speechless!

Guide book: J.M Pearson's Canal Companion: Welsh Waters - www.jmpearson.co.uk/

APRIL CANAL WALKING

From Cheshire into Shropshire
From Shropshire into Wales
Walking to Llangollen
The beauty never fails
Beside canal lay sprinkled
Primrose and celandine
Perfect yellow petals
The earthen path to line
Starbursts of hawthorn blossom
Fresh drapes of willow green
Birdsong in the hedgerows
All grace this country scene
Pairs of ducks a-floating
Close by each ardent drake
Time to be a-breeding
A hidden nest to make
Pure white the wood anemone
Across the wayside spills
Reflected in calm waters
The waving daffodils

Along a quiet section
Cowslips spring a surprise
While from a hidden waterway
A startled heron flies
High up in the budding trees
The long-tailed tits at play
Chiff-chaffs a background soundtrack
To gentle April day.

CANAL CRISS-CROSS

Criss-crossing to Llangollen
Towpath on left or right
Finding out which side to walk
When bridges come in sight
Mile on mile unrolling
As walkers hold their course
Canal a silvery ribbon
Reflecting vibrant gorse
Past junction to Montgomery
Welsh hills come into view
From fields the bleat of new-born lambs
As narrowboats pass through

Buds on branches bursting
Trees clothed in fresh leaf green
Flowers in profusion
The path heads on between
Ahead the long Chirk Tunnel
A quarter mile of gloom
No fun for the faint-hearted
Who fear there waits their doom
A hand rail's placed for safety
At centre it's near black
Even those with head torch find
Once in no turning back
Then on towards Llangollen
Where far above the Dee
There stands the famous aqueduct
Which thousands come to see
Eighteen vast stone arches
One, twenty-six feet high
Another Telford masterpiece
That dominates the sky.

THE MACMILLAN WAY
Boston to Abbotsbury – 290 miles

The ancient Lincolnshire town of Boston, once a prosperous seaport on the edge of the Fens, has always been a starting point for journeys and indeed it was hardy seafaring folk from there, who sailed out across the Atlantic in the 1630s to found the city of Boston, Massachusetts.

Today it is the starting point for another long journey, not aided by the wind and tide, but by a sturdy pair of legs and stout sticks and blown along by a love of exploring our amazingly-beautiful English countryside.

This 290-mile journey is the Macmillan Way. created by the Macmillan Way Association in support of the cancer relief charity, which does so much to help those afflicted with this 21st Century scourge.

A wonderful aspect of this journey, which roughly follows the rich Cotswold stone belt all the way across country to the South Coast at Abbotsbury in Dorset, is that it only passes through three towns, namely Stamford in Lincolnshire, Cirencester in Gloucestershire and Sherborne in Dorset.

So, for all those miles, the way follows field paths and country lanes, through woodland and by small rivers and quiet streams, pausing delightfully now and again to pass through quiet villages where, if one is lucky, there is a shop for supplies, or even better, a warm welcome in a friendly inn.

Most of us do not have the luxury of time to undertake a 290-mile trek all in one go, so what better way than to divide the Macmillan trail up into two or three-day sections.

In that way one can return to the walk at regular intervals and journey ever onward through the gradually-changing vistas of the rural counties of Lincolnshire, Northamptonshire, Warwickshire, Gloucestershire, Wiltshire, Somerset, Devon and lastly Dorset, in all the seasons of the year.

So, one Spring morning, Peter, and I set out from Boston's White Hart Hotel and spent many a happy day walking across the landscape, under ever-changing skies, appreciating the scenery, finding sheltered or sunny spots for snacks and looking forward to a hearty evening dinner and friendly company.

Every so often, the fabric of the buildings showed the presence of the golden stone strata, which the Macmillan Way follows across the country and which is more often associated with much of Gloucestershire and Oxfordshire.

Covering a hillside, Stamford has the reputation of being the 'finest stone town in England' and after a night's stay we strolled out along a delightful green vale beside the meandering River Welland and came to a bridge.

It was here in AD 61 that the survivors of the Ninth Roman Legion fled the vengeful warrior queen, Boudicca.

A little further on, we came to the small village of Ketton with its distinctive railway signal box, immortalised by Hornby in model train sets found throughout the world.

Then there was the Rutland morning we found a sunny seat for a break, besides which was a box of plants and an honesty box. We had not been there long when a lady appeared from a nearby cottage and offered us mugs of coffee.

It was the first time we had ever received such generosity, so we left our flasks in our sacks and willingly accepted her kind offer.

Not far from Market Harborough in Northamptonshire, we toiled up the long road into Great Brington, following the estate wall of Althorp Park, the family seat of Earl Spencer, to find the village post office and shop full of Princess Diana memorabilia.

Further along the way and passing through a lovely section of Cotswold countryside, we found ourselves in the sleepy village of Adlestrop, made famous by the poet Edward Thomas, whose train happened to stop there on Brunel's London to Worcester railway line.

"Yes, I remember Adlestrop," is the opening sentence of his short poem about this delightfully-rural idyll, but sadly he was killed in action during the Battle of Arras in 1917, soon after arriving in France

Shortly afterwards, we passed the picturesque rectory, often visited by Jane Austen when her uncle, Theophilus Leigh, lived there and stopped for a break resting against a fallen tree in open parkland.

Then there was the afternoon we found shelter in a country church porch, took off our rucksacks and dripping coats and stretched out on an old coconut mat to rest awhile.

We must have looked like a couple of vagrants, when a couple carrying a bouquet appeared and were obviously surprised to see their way blocked in such a disagreeable manner.

We discovered that they had been married there 40 years ago and had travelled up from Somerset to commemorate the occasion.

And then there was the pub, where muddy boots were welcome, and another where we arrived weary on a November evening to find mine host and his lady wife in the middle of a blazing row.

We stayed in a country house, where we were offered glasses of wine in front of blazing log fire, cosy oak-beamed cottages and in many a modern family home.

And it was not for the first time that an obliging host drove us a mile or so to a pub or restaurant, either to save our legs or from getting another soaking.

In Cirencester we stopped at a bakery for our elevenses and when the owner discovered we were on the Macmillan Way she gave us each a cake.

"Well now we've been given the 'freebun' of Cirencester," said Peter.

Moving slowly ever westward along byways and field paths, we came down to picture-postcard Castle Combe, on the edge of the Cotswolds, often named the prettiest village in England, and having now walked through many villages on our way, I do not think I can really disagree with that description.

From there, we made our way to the historic Saxon town of Bradford-on-Avon, before plodding up onto higher ground en route to the pretty Somerset village of Mells, famous for its fine architecture and ancient streets.

We now walked on to Frome, built on higher ground at the eastern end of the Mendip Hills and beyond to the smaller market town of Bruton on the meandering River Brue.

On entering nearby Castle Cary, there was a decision to be made because it is here that the Macmillan Way divides with a 102-mile arm heading west through South Somerset and over the Quantock Hills and Dunkery Beacon, the highest point on Exmoor, to finish on the North Devon coast at Barnstaple.

Peter and I decide to head west and were not disappointed because, having plodded through the vast flatness of the famous flood-prone Somerset Levels, we made our way up and over the wooded and rolling Quantock Hills and down across the fringes of Exmoor to finish in the medieval village of Dunster, near Minehead.

Here we decided to stop and head back to Castle Cary for the final few days walking to Sherborne, which, nestling in green valleys and wooded hills and mainly built of mellow stone, is one of the most picturesque medieval towns in England

Ahead lay the final 30-mile walk, passing to the west of busy Dorchester and coming at last to the Jurassic Coast at Abbotsbury, where we admired the view over the sparkling sea with the end of the Chesil Beach below and the sunlit isle of Portland far off to the left.

Before reaching this journey's end and very close to the coast on an open hillside, a final treat was in store when we came upon two hares boxing - so intent was the female in holding off her male suiter that they failed no notice us for several minutes.

But did this really have to be the end of the walk we asked ourselves while enjoying a celebratory evening dinner in a nearby hotel - because, after all, the famous South West Coast Path, which at 630 miles is the UK's longest trail, was now right on our doorstep!

Guide book: The Macmillan Way - www.macmillanway.org/

Our Macmillan Way Extension

So began yet another long-distance walk, first along the Jurassic Coast, as far as Exmouth, and this was certainly to be a strenuous section, with us toiling up and up on sheer cliffs and then plunging right down to sea-level again.

From Burton Bradstock and West Bay, we plodded up to Golden Cap, which at 191 metres, is arguably the highest point on the South Coast.

Walking along close to the top on a glorious summer morning, we were making our way slowly towards a seat that was going to afford us the most amazing views, while we enjoyed our sandwich lunch.

"What I can't understand, Peter, is that we have seen no one for ages, so where are all the retired people, who must have plenty of time to go walking?"

No sooner were the words out of my mouth, when an elderly couple emerged from a side path and took our seat!

Now we walked down into the hamlet of Seatown, with its small beach, one of the local coastal meccas for fossil hunters, and then up again and onward to the picturesque Victorian resort of Lyme Regis.

The town and surrounding wooded hills, are renowned for their natural beauty and it is also famous as the birthplace of Mary Anning, a renowned fossil collector and palaeontologist.

We stopped for refreshments at a café on the promenade and were seated outside in the sunshine, when Peter turned to the couple sitting next to us.

"Excuse me, but do you by any chance have an antiques shop in Oxford?" he asked. "I do," the somewhat surprised lady replied.

"And does your husband restore furniture?" he enquired. "He does," she responded. "Well, I think I sat next to you at a jazz brunch in Oxfordshire," Peter explained.

We stayed in a B&B overnight and then set out on the famous seven-mile Undercliff walk to Axmouth, which is a sheltered wooded wilderness through one of the most active coastal landslide systems in Western Europe.

It is a fascinating natural habitat, said to be the closest walkers can get to a rainforest in the UK, with a warm and humid micro-climate, supporting carpets of ferns beneath a leafy canopy of ash and other trees.

It was indeed a memorable experience, we agreed, as we made our way through Axmouth and walked on to Seaton and then to the small picture-postcard village of Beer, with its sheltered cove and colourful fishing boats drawn up above the tide line.

We stayed in a B&B overnight and continued on along the undulating coast path and finally steeply down into Regency Sidmouth, with its beautiful gardens and fine hotels, which became the place to stay during Queen Victoria's reign.

Now our way continued around the sweep of Ladram Bay and on to Budleigh Salterton, once nicknamed Poonah Town, because of the number of expats, who settled there from India in the closing years of the British Empire.

We were now within striking distance of the seaside resort of Exmouth, on the east bank of the River Exe, and finished this stage with a walk across the long sandy beach stretched out in front of the town.

From the opposite side of the river, on our return visit, we made our way through many a leafy lane to join the fabulously-scenic Two Moors Way, linking Dartmoor with Exmoor.

This often, breathtaking walk finishes on the coast at picturesque Lynmouth, surrounded by steeply-rising and wooded hills.

But the highlight of our chosen route, was an overnight stay in the pretty Exmoor town of Dulverton and a delightful walk up the River Barle, passing the Tarr Steps beauty spot and on to the lovely village of Withypool, right in the heart of the Exmoor National Park.

Luckily, there was a B&B, close to the warm and cosy Royal Oak Inn, where we dined on Barnsley Chops, of course, not knowing that one day we would be staying in that South Yorkshire market town, while walking the Leeds and Liverpool Canal.

Off early the following morning, we continued upriver and through a wild and remote area, surrounded by moorland hills, until we levelled out on higher ground and decided on a change of plan.

No, we would not continue across the moorland and down the steeply-wooded valleys into Lynmouth, but divert through a series of quiet country lanes to Barnstaple on the River Taw, the largest town in North Devon.

Here, we rejoined our old friend, the South West Coast Path and followed it to the North Devon seaside resort of Woolacombe, with its two-mile-long gently sloping sandy beach, facing the Atlantic Ocean, near its western limits with the Bristol Channel.

From here we followed on a mostly high-level footpath, with magnificent views out over the channel to Lundy Island and the distant Welsh coastline, to come at last to picturesque Ilfracombe with its small sheltered harbour surrounded by high hills.

Ilfracombe was a popular destination in the days when dozens of paddle steamers brought thousands of day trippers down channel from Bristol, Clevedon and Weston-super-Mare and over from South Wales.

Not far beyond Ilfracombe, we dropped down into a small wooded inlet, called Heddon's Mouth, where a fascinating World War Two story came to mind. For it was here that German U-boats operating in the Bristol Channel would surface in the dead of night to collect fresh water.

Now a long and quite strenuous walk brought us to Lynmouth, which marks the starting point of the Two Moors Way from which we'd earlier departed high on Exmoor.

"I think I've had enough of coastal walking," I said to Peter over supper in a harbourside restaurant.

I was thinking ahead to the following day when another long and quite strenuous, mostly high-level walk, would bring us at last to our final journey's end at pretty Porlock in Somerset.

The alternative, definitely a no-brainer, at this stage, was to follow the picturesque path up the fast-flowing East Lyn river to the famous Watersmeet beauty spot and beyond to the tiny hamlet of Rockford.

A couple of miles further on, the path leads out to a peaceful valley, amid high hills, and onto a mostly quiet road, which we followed to the entrance of the Doone Valley, made famous by R.J. Blackmore in his novel, Lorna Doone.

Further on, our road became a single track, winding its way up to the main A39, linking Porlock with Ilfracombe, and not far from the infamously-steep Porlock Hill.

From here we chose the easier toll road into Porlock, but soon branching off down a series of steeply-sloping woodland paths to come at last to our final journey's end in pretty Porlock Weir.

A few years later, we would be meeting ourselves walking down to Watersmeet on the Coleridge Way.

NATURE'S PICTURE PATCHWORK

From Lincolnshire to Dorset
From Stump to Swannery
They walked the fine Macmillan Way
From Wash to English Sea
With book and Ordnance Survey
They found the waymarked routes
And stickers left on posts and stiles
Were there to guide their boots
They stayed in modest B&Bs
And country houses grand
Their gear in rucksacks on their backs
And each stop carefully planned
Through villages and hamlets
Down paths and bridleways
Their passage marked across the land
By ever-changing days
Felt Autumn fade to Winter chill
Saw Spring's green shoots appear
Stopped at pubs in Summer heat
To slake their thirst with beer

Heard larks ascending skywards
Watched hares and rabbits run
Saw timid deer take instant flight
And hawks backlit by sun
The seasons' floral calendar
Gave scents to woodland scenes
Of bluebells and wild garlic
And buttercup-lined streams

From snowdrops in a hidden dell
To blossom's multi-hue
From poppy red to campion pink
And petals flecked with dew
From tall bullrush and lilies
To moorland gorse and heather
Nature's picture patchwork
As changing as the weather
They sheltered under hedgerows
As wind whipped overhead
Slumbered in the sunshine
With soft grass as their bed
Battled over new-ploughed fields
To reach a distant gate
Warmed themselves on evenings
Before a glowing grate

With waterproofs and gaiters
They braved the lashing rain
Trudging through a sea of mud
Another mile to gain
Met characters and kindnesses
With buns and cups of tea
Glimpsed unhurried rural life
That few are blessed to see
Entered country churches
With timeless peace within
Rushed across wide motorways
To leave their ceaseless din
They left the Wash on river banks
Where cattle sought the breeze
Retreating to the lower ground
When bulls rose from their knees
From Stamford spires to Rutland
And waters filled with trout
And onward cross the landscape
With scarce a soul about
Parkland known by Austen
A station caught in rhyme
Savouring these echoes
Of England's gentler time
Northamptonshire to Warwickshire
And then the Cotswold heights
Gloucestershire to Wiltshire
Enjoying ramblers' rights
In Somerset a side trail
To link with far Exmoor
But after reaching Dunster
They turned back for the shore
That beckoned them in Dorset
Through lanes to Abbotsbury
Where green fields merged with beaches -
At last the shining sea.

BAUNTON IN JANUARY

With muddy boots and rucksacks
The walkers stepped within
The tiny church at Baunton
It surely was no sin
To gaze upon St Christopher
The travellers' patron saint
His features warmly visible
In 14th century paint
Though time had colours faded
From their once vivid hue
The message still was clear to see
The meaning still shone through

Upon his sturdy shoulders
The Christ child safely borne
Across the raging torrent
Protected from the storm
The image faithfully rendered
'Fore Shakespeare conjured words
And Man would leave the solid earth
To fly among the birds

Outside the walls lay snowdrops
Inside a quiet calm
The walkers left on tip toe
Lest carpets they should harm
In the porch a notice
To welcome a new priest
Soon to bring his flock along
To share in God's great feast.

THE OXFORD CANAL
Coventry to Oxford – 78 miles

It is often said there is more in heaven and earth than we shall ever know and so it seemed as we stepped out on a January winter walking adventure along the Oxford Canal.

Right out of the blue Peter, who had been researching his Gibbs family tree, received an email from a fellow enthusiast saying she was distantly related to him.

She lived in a small village, called Cropredy, near Banbury, that he had never heard of, but then, when adding a day to extend our walk's stage, he discovered to his amazement it was where we would end up for a night's stay.

Chatting to people we meet and gaining a snapshot of their lives is all part of the adventure for us and we were instantly rewarded on arriving at the Hawkesbury Junction with the Coventry Canal, the official start of the 78-mile walk to Oxford.

Just assembling, like yellow-jacketed bees around their white van, were volunteer members of the Canal & River Trust's North Warwickshire, Coventry and Ashby Towpath Taskforce.

It is bands of enthusiasts like these, who spend days weed-clearing, litter-picking, planting, painting, and doing many other maintenance jobs, that keep Britain's wonderful network of canals open for all to enjoy.

A day's steady walking passing under the giant portals of the M69 and then the M6 and through miles of open countryside brought us in the gathering gloom to the Barley Mow pub, right on the canal side at Newbold-on-Avon, where we were staying the night.

We received a friendly, if not slightly curious, welcome from the locals as we entered with our heavy rucksacks and walking poles and with our map cases slung around our necks.

But I was the more surprised when, after taking off my waterproofs, I entered the Gents to find an upright piano sitting next to the urinals.

"Was it time for a tinkle on the ivories?" I wondered.

The piano, it seemed, had been parked there during a pub refurbishment, but then was found to be too heavy to move without damaging the floor, so now it had become a permanent feature and even played at times - the acoustics being rather good, I was told.

As we always leave at dawn, it was too early for breakfast, but assistance materialised when a lady appeared from around the corner of one of the many lovely red brick canal bridges to tell us that a few paces further on a footpath led to a supermarket with a cafe.

We were now walking through Rugby, which has made the most of the underside of some of these bridges by creating mosaic-style art depicting both the town's sporting and barge transport history.

Another delightful day's walking under clear blue skies brought us to Braunston dominated by the impressive spire of All Saints Church, romantically known as the Cathedral of the Canals because it stands at the junction of the Oxford Canal with the Grand Union, linking London with Birmingham.

Here we took a taxi to a hotel, because it was too far to walk, and then returned to Napton-on-the-Hill the following morning to continue the walk to Cropredy, where Peter had arranged to meet his newly-discovered relative.

We had skipped the six miles from Braunston to Napton, having covered that section while walking the Grand Union Canal the previous winter.

Now the canal wound its way around higher ground affording vistas of rolling sheep-flecked hills and as we approached journey's end, we were suddenly reminded of the recent death of Cuban leader Fidel Castro.

For painted on the end of a narrow boat, was a striking image of his famous compatriot, Che Guevara.

Then, following a convivial evening with Peter's relative, Sue, and her husband, Martyn and a comfortable night's stay at the Brasenose Arms, we returned to find the canal covered in a thin layer of ice and swirling mist.

So began a swift, body-warming march into famous Banbury, which ended with us entering a coffee shop and bursting into Donovan's famous song, Mellow Yellow.

The reason - the lady who served us was called Saffron and she'd never heard how keen the pop star was about her namesake.

Having consulted our Ordnance Survey map and seen there was no lunch-time hostelry on the long stretch to our next overnight stop at Aynho Wharf, we made a country lane diversion to the pretty village of King's Sutton and were rewarded with hot food and log fires.

We received an equally warm winter welcome at the Great Western Arms at Aynho Wharf and spent a happy time learning about the lives of three 'temporary' locals, who were over wintering there on their boats.

It was a real pleasure to experience the landscape opening up the following morning, as we trekked through the Cherwell Valley in company with the meandering River Cherwell and to come across a Canal and River Trust workman.

He was busy assisting with the re-filling of a section of the canal, which had been drained as part of a maintenance operation.

More social experiences were in store, after the disappointing discovery that the Lower Heyford hostelry would not be opening for another half hour!

For as, with hearts in our boots, we turned away, we immediately spotted a sign for a pop-up cafe in the village church and were warmly welcomed, muddy boots and all.

Here we passed a memorable hour with villagers and their part-time priest, Geoff Price, and his authoress wife, Hope, who had spent their early lives doing missionary work in Africa.

Our overnight stay was in Kirtlington, which we left at 7am for the final walk into Oxford.

And as the sun burst through the icy gloom for the first time in several days, I was reminded of the Rev Price's parting words to us.

"Remember St Augustine said: 'Praise the Lord and Keep on Walking.'"

Guide book: J.M Pearson's Canal Companion: Oxford and Grand Union and Upper Thames - www.jmpearson.co.uk/

CROPREDY MEAL

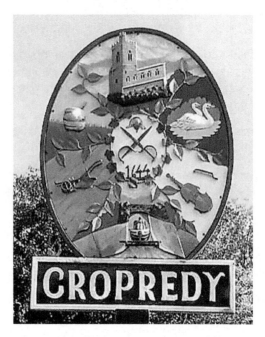

When of the village Cropredy
The folk fans hear a mention
They know it is the place to find
The band Fairport Convention
Who hold an annual festival
But I had never known
That this was where a relative
Would invite to her home
A welcome stop along canal
That in the Midlands starts
And ends in heart of city famed
For science and the arts.

THE OXFORDSHIRE WAY
Bourton-on-the-Water to Henley-on-Thames – 68 miles

Setting out on one of Britain's long-distance footpaths is to embark on an adventure, never quite knowing, what lies ahead, and so it was with Oxfordshire Way.

This is a wonderful walk, through quintessential English countryside, with picturesque villages all along the whole of its 68 miles from Bourton-on-the-Water in the Cotswolds, to Henley-on-Thames.

But before I begin waxing too lyrical, Peter and I started trudging out of this Cotswold tourist spot in a downpour, slowly beginning to cook in our heavy waterproofs, with raindrops making it difficult to read the map in its plastic cover.

Beyond the lovely village of Wyck Rissington, the way rises to meet the busy A424 and then we regained the path as it descended though deciduous woodland, cloaked in billions of fresh green leaves.

A deer crossed the trail ahead and then amazingly so did a walker, who we had met briefly in an hotel that morning, but he was following The Diamond Way Cotswold walk

Later, the sun came out and off came the waterproofs, so increasing the load on our backs, but our boots and gaiters were caked in mud and also had to come off before entering the village pub beside the green at Bledington for lunch.

Resuming the walk, we paused at a corner to puzzle out the way ahead and were looking at our Ordnance Survey map when a villager appeared and offered to help.

"I've got as much bigger map than that," he said beckoning us to follow him into his cottage, where, to our surprise, we saw he had actually papered a whole wall with one!

That afternoon, we walked through parkland in the hamlet of Bruern Abbey, beside the meandering River Evenlode and had now left Gloucestershire for Oxfordshire.

With a whole panorama of views ahead, in a day's unfolding landscape, studded with dazzling yellow fields of rape seed, which left a slightly acrid scent on the air, we made our way to our night's stopover at The Swan in Ascott-under-Wychwood in the Evenlode Valley.

Early the following morning, we set out on a fabulous day's sunlit walk, which included mostly long, straight and usually uncomplicated sections along the wide Evenlode Valley.

By noon, we were climbing the hill into the attractive mellow-stoned village of Charlbury, where bright sunlight was casting black shadows onto the roads, and could not resist popping into The Bull to slake our thirst.

From there, a woodland track, carpeted with spring flowers, stretched ahead for several miles and we left it midway to munch our sandwiches on the edge of a field with fine views.

Quite suddenly the small and delightful village of Stonesfield appeared on an escarpment ahead, and after climbing a steep path to enter it, we came across two mums chatting, who gave us directions to the village shop for ice lollies.

Retracing our steps to pass through the village churchyard, we were soon descending a steep and rocky path to come upon the River Evenlode, which had been our faithful, yet often distant, companion over many a mile.

But we were not to cross it because just yards from the water, the Oxfordshire Way quickly picks up the Akeman Street Roman road.

Now only the occasional cursory glance at the map was needed on that warm late afternoon, as we followed its track for several miles in a true-to-form, dead straight line, to enter the Blenheim Palace estate, via a steep footbridge over the tall boundary wall.

Suddenly we recalled climbing those very steps, five years earlier, when walking the Shakespeare's Way from Stratford-upon-Avon to London's iconic Globe Theatre, where we had been given a back-stage show-round.

Beyond the manicured, tree-studded, parkland, it was an hour's walk on to our night's accommodation at Sturdy's Castle, a most welcome stopover hostelry on the busy A4260.

Saying farewell to Akeman Street, we crossed the Oxford Canal, which is another wonderful 78-mile walk linking the university town with Coventry and is also featured in this book.

Now, we continued through the quiet villages of Kirtlington, Weston-on-the-Green and Islip, where we stopped for lunch, before heading on to the delightful hamlet of Noke with its duck pond.

Moving, ever onward, to Beckley, we had a cuppa in a pub garden and were amused to find the village's red telephone box being used for an art display.

Then, topping a rise, we were afforded our first panoramic view over the Thames Valley, before descending to a dull stretch of farmland and on to our next overnight stop at Waterperry Common.

On our fourth day, we twice crossed the busy M40 as it looped our trail to lunch in a pub beside the cricket pitch in Tetworth.

Early that afternoon, and again gasping for a cuppa, we arrived in Pyrton, only to find the pub had closed seventeen years ago, but was that not a brass band playing?

Drawn forward, Pied Piper fashion, we found the village fete in full-swing and were soon queuing up for tea and cake.

Later with the wooded slopes of the Chilterns Hills ridge rising out of the landscape ahead of us, we had another deja vu moment on suddenly crossing the Greater Ridgeway path which we had also completed some years ago.

As Britain's longest inland trail, it covers 363 miles from Lyme Regis in Dorset to the sea at Hunstanton in Norfolk.

It was now a comparatively short, but steep climb to reach the Chilterns ridge before descending through more woodlands, awash with bluebells and wild garlic, to reach our final overnight stop at Pishill.

The seven-mile walk into Henley-on-Thames the following morning has to be one of the finest finales of any long-distance English trail, taking in country lanes, more wonderful woodland, and magnificent parkland on a plateau above the town.

Guide book: The Oxfordshire Way, A Walkers Guide, published by CPRE Oxfordshire - www.cpreoxon.org.uk/countryside/the-oxfordshire-way/

CRISS-CROSSING HISTORY

A beginning in the Cotswolds
Immersed in golden stone
To end in bustling Henley
On paths oft' walked alone
Criss-crossing ways of history
Where Roman legions trod
Byways linking churches
To lead plain folk to God
Past Blenheim's famous palace
Where Churchill first saw light
Like first Duke of Marlborough
Not shy to go and fight
Then sojourn at a village fete
Where welcomed like a friend
Before the lofty Chilterns
And down to Thames descend.

THE SEVERN WAY
Llanidloes to Aust – 220 miles

It was a late sunny afternoon in autumn and Peter and I were walking along a quiet country lane on our way to Ironbridge in Shropshire.

We were on the magnificent Severn Way national trail, which runs from the source of Britain's longest river in mid-Wales to the Severn Bridge at Aust, near Bristol.

I just happened to glance across to the opposite verge and spotted what looked like a tea plate.

My first thought was that it was made of paper, but when I picked it up and turned it over, I saw that it was made of delicate bone china with a lovely pattern around its edge.

Thinking up explanations as to how it came to be there occupied us as we trudged wearily into Ironbridge in the gathering gloom and luckily chanced upon a small tea shop.

A little bell tinkled as we entered and took off our heavy packs, only to be told by the owner that she had just closed, but when she saw the look of disappointment on our tired faces she relented and offered us a couple of mugs of tea.

We got chatting as we tucked into delicious cupcakes and on an impulse, I showed her our tea plate, which I had intended giving to my wife, Jenny.

The owner loved the plate, so we made her a present of it and received two more cakes in a little box to see us on our way.

It was dark when we set out again and made our way past the world's first iron bridge, built across the Severn in 1779 and now a famous tourist attraction, and found the inn where we were booked in for the night.

Surprisingly, china plates were suddenly very much back on our minds the following morning when, shortly after setting out, we suddenly found our riverside way blocked by what looked like a massive earth-moving operation.

Luckily, we spotted a man in a hard hat fixing a notice to a tree.

He explained that thousands of tons of discarded plates and tiles from former industrial potteries had been dumped beside the works and after many years, the whole lot had started sliding down the river bank, which now had to be stabilised.

We were much relieved when he pointed out the diversion, which had been created for walkers, and were soon on our way.

Our journey down the Severn Way had begun in the spring of 2014, when, equipped with our customary waterproofs, sturdy boots, handy walking poles and backpacks carrying our overnight gear, lunch and water, we set out from Llanidloes in Powys.

From this charming mid-Wales market town, it is good day's walk up through the Hafren Forest to the source of the Severn, which rises at an altitude of 2,001 feet on boggy and marshy moorland at Plynlimon.

But as I had done this out-and-back section some years earlier and, as we always tell ourselves – we're not purists - we made Llanidloes the start of our walk.

On the first and most strenuous sections of the Severn Way, we spent little time by the river, as the path meanders through magnificent mid-Wales countryside.

From Llanidloes, we made our way to the village of Caersws, a settlement since Roman times, and from there on to attractive Newtown on the banks of the Upper Severn, where we joined the Montgomery Canal and so on to Welshpool.

After saying farewell to this picturesque riverside community, we had rejoined the canal for a while before leaving Wales and entering Shropshire en route to Shrewsbury and so on to Ironbridge and the mystery plate.

Another day's gentle walking, mostly by the river, brought us to Bridgnorth, which is perched spectacularly on top of a sandstone cliff and is the end of the line for the Severn Valley Steam Railway.

This makes a great starting point for anyone wishing to sample the Severn Way, because they can easily spend a day walking through delightful water meadows, accompanied by occasional glimpses of the train, stay overnight in Bewdley, another most attractive Severnside town, and catch the train back in the morning.

From here the way remains faithfully by the Severn as it meanders on to historic, Worcester, Tewkesbury and Gloucester, where in each case, two magnificent cathedrals and one lovely old abbey are welcome landmarks for weary walkers reaching the end of yet another day.

From Gloucester another three days' steady walking by a now ever-widening river brought us at last to the open reaches of the Severn Estuary and a most welcome sight - the Grade 1-listed Severn Bridge.

Guide book: Cicerone Guides' Severn Way by Terry Marsh - www.cicerone.co.uk/.

SEVERN SOURCE TO SILVER SEA

From trickling stream in village
Where ducks are daily fed
Ever southwards, ever onward
Their footsteps surely led
The pure Welsh rain sustaining
The source in hidden vale
A very small beginning
For Severn's mighty tale
The hills of Wales behind them
Ahead a Shropshire gorge
Where thanks to Telford's genius
An iron bridge was forged
Then on to shadow railway
Fulfillment of a dream
By those who mourn what once was known
As golden age of steam
The waterway expanding
The towns and hamlets passed
Then on through Gloucester city
'Til estuary reached at last

Where silvered sandbanks caught the light
Beneath a cloudless sky
Feeding ground for waders
But hid when tide is high
Curlews searched for morsels
While up above gulls called
All there to reap this bonus
Left by the tidal fall
Between its shores in Gloucestershire
The river flowed to sea
Below the double bridges link
To Principality.

SHAKESPEARE'S AVON WAY
Naseby to Tewkesbury – 88 miles

The Northamptonshire village of Naseby has a claim to fame other than being the site of the famous English Civil War battle between Charles 1st's Cavaliers and Oliver Cromwell's New Model Army.

For the River Avon rises here and makes it the start of Shakespeare's Avon Way, an 88-mile national trail meandering into neighbouring Warwickshire and Worcestershire before reaching its confluence with the River Severn at Tewkesbury in Gloucestershire.

Peter and I completed this walk in six and a half days having small adventures along the way, including picnicking by accident in a private garden and meeting a young Polish World Kick Boxing Champion.

Setting out from the village's Lion War Memorial, we soon branched off into rolling, crop-filled, open country and made our first footbridge crossing of the infant Avon.

By lunch time we'd entered St Andrew's Churchyard in the hamlet of Clay Coton and because there were no seats, we picnicked on the grass.

Peter was munching a sandwich when he read in our guide book that this was a redundant church and now a private house and at that very moment the owner appeared to confirm that we were indeed sitting on his lawn!

But he was good natured about it, explaining that the 12th century church had fallen into ruin before being restored by a local builder.

We'd walked under overcast skies all morning, but by mid-afternoon it was sweltering, so we popped into The Bull in Clifton-upon-Dunsmore for a refresher.

Underpass mural in Rugby

Revived, we strolled down into a wooded valley to join the Oxford Canal and followed it into Rugby for our overnight stay.

Back on the canal, we came across a pair of swans and their cygnets around a pub sandwich board as if studying the menu.

By the time we were lunching in a pub garden at Bretford, we'd crossed the landscape on a series of well-marked paths without a soul in sight.

Now we walked on to Wolston, via a wonderful brick-arched Victorian railway tunnel under the Coventry-to-Rugby line and soon linked up with the Coventry and Centenary Ways, which we followed to Ryton-on-Dunsmore.

By late afternoon we'd reached Bubbenhall from where a taxi took us to a local hotel for the night.

Some miles beyond the village the following morning, we came upon some ugly metal fences, seemingly in the middle of nowhere.

All was revealed by dog walkers, who explained that this was the route of the controversial HS2 line and that half their South Cubbington bluebell wood was to be destroyed to make way for it.

132

The heavens opened as we followed the wooded River Leam into Leamington and then on to the famous castle-dominated town of Warwick where we spent the night.

The way out of town led along the Grand Union Canal, where memories of a previous much-enjoyed canal walk came to mind, although neither Peter nor I could remember this particular section.

The thing is that we have now walked through, and stayed in, so many villages across the country over the years, that when one happens to pop up and is pictured on the TV, more often than not, I am left with a deja vu feeling because I know I have been there before, but simply can't remember where it is or when it was.

Leaving the canal beyond the spectacular Hatton Flight of locks, we soon came to Hampton-on-the Hill where another surprise was in store.

For on opening the parish magazine in the Roman Catholic Church of St Charles Borremeo, Peter spotted a picture of the former Royal Pier Hotel in his home town of Clevedon on the Bristol Channel, where I also spent my childhood.

All was revealed on reading that Lord of the Rings author JRR Tolkien was married in a sister church in Warwick, but spent his honeymoon in our Victorian seaside town.

Now we encountered quite a difficult cross-country section, along a series of heavily-overgrown paths, with the way being difficult to follow in places.

I'd rolled up my trekking trouser legs as the morning heated up, but was now being attacked by prickly wheat stalks and stinging nettles as we trudged up the side of a huge field, alive with tiny butterflies and buzzing with insects.

Emerging onto a quiet country lane, we walked into Hampton Lucy, where refreshing pints of lime and soda were downed at The Boars Head before making our way back to the River Avon.

Now high on a hill we spotted the Welcome Monument, a spectacular obelisk erected by a local family of merchants, and enjoyed our final flask cuppa there before moving on to find Shakespeare's house in busy and tourist bustling Stratford-upon-Avon.

After overnighting, we donned full waterproofs to follow the nine-mile-long Avon River Walk to Bidford-on-Avon, where we would later stay overnight while walking the Heart of England Way.

Here on crossing the centuries-old bridge we spotted a sandwich board for a cafe and were drawn to it like bedraggled bees to a sheltering honeypot.

It stopped raining as we walked through water meadows and across a landscape now dominated by huge glasshouses in the famously fertile Vale of Evesham.

And here in this picturesque riverside town, another surprise was in store after we'd checked into an hotel only to be served at the bar by a former Polish world champion kickboxer, who'd moved to Evesham to be close to a member of her family.

The bells of Fladbury Church rang out across the vale the following morning, calling us to our coffee stop on the village green.

Ahead, lay a series of tracks across pasture land with our first distant views of the Malvern Hills and beyond, journey's end in Tewkesbury.

After Fladbury, we reached the curiously-named village of Wyre Piddle before strolling into the lovely riverside town of Pershore for lunch.

There was no way we'd complete the twelve miles into Tewkesbury so we walked on to picturesque Great Comberton, where Peter's parents were married and locals look after the nearby quay, also using their telephone box as a lending library.

Here we taxied back to Pershore for our overnight stay and then out again to resume the walk with the last three miles into Tewkesbury being through riverside water meadows under clear blue skies and an absolute delight.

Guide book: Shakespeare's Avon Way published by The Shakespeare's Way Association - www.shakespearesway.org/

SHAKESPEARE'S WAY WITH THE AVON

River Avons can be found
Up and down the land
Sometimes when looking at a map
It's hard to understand
But Shakespeare's Avon is unique
What makes it stand apart
Like Britain's war uncivil
In Naseby is its start
From just a little trickle
Then stream, it surely grows
As down through orchard country
Towards the South it flows
Past Evesham As You Like It
To Be Or Not To Be
Overlooked by abbey
It ends in Tewkesbury.

SHAKESPEARE'S WAY
Stratford-upon-Avon to The Globe, London – 146 miles

There are three reasons why walking Shakespeare's Way stands out in our memories, like church spires in the landscape of the past.

This 146-mile trail linking the bard's home in Stratford-upon-Avon with the famous Globe Theatre beside the River Thames in the heart of London, follows a route which the poet and playwright might well have taken.

It is without doubt one of the most picturesque country walks we have done and just thinking about it now tempts me to say to Peter,' let's go and do it again,' but, of course, that's never going to happen.

This is the point where I lift my head towards the sky and hope that our Cosmic Joker is not listening!

Anyway, not to digress any further, Shakespeare's Way sets out along the valley of the River Stour to the Warwickshire village of Cherington and here we met a lady, who remembered when Peter recreated Ambridge in their village for a day.

He turned their pub into The Bull and peopled it with more than a dozen actors from the long-running radio serial as part of a Western Daily Press competition, which invited readers to win a coach trip to the fictional Ambridge.

From Cherington, and ticking off the first of our three memories, the way climbs up and over the rolling landscape of the Oxfordshire Cotswolds and down to the busy market town of Chipping Norton, one of our night stop-overs.

Now we made our way along a series of lovely wooded valleys and through magnificent Blenheim Park to Woodstock and the scene of our second memory, namely the quiet church at Bladon where Sir Winston Churchill is buried.

I was expecting some grand memorial, but no, his last resting place and that of his beloved wife, Clementine, was marked with a simple flat stone.

What a contrast to a tomb we encountered later on the walk inside the parish church in the pretty village of Hambleden near Henley-on-Thames.

Here local landowner, Sir Cope D'Oyley, who died in 1633, is commemorated in an elaborate marble monument, showing him kneeling in prayer facing his wife, Martha, with their five sons alongside him and their five daughters alongside her.

It was a few days' previously, before joining the River Thames and on our way into bustling Oxford that we were taught a lesson, which prompted our third memory of the walk - the lesson being the need to always carry a small first aid kit!

For it was while we were walking behind a small untidy complex of buildings that Peter caught the top of his head on a branch and, even though he was wearing a baseball hat, the metal stud on the top of it delivered a nasty gash.

The heavens opened when we reached Oxford, so we took shelter in a nearby pub and had lunch, after which the sun came out as we made our way through busy streets to regain the Thames path, which we followed for several miles out into peaceful open country.

Now the way led steadily upwards onto the wooded Chilterns escarpment and then forward crossing several valleys to be reunited with the River Thames at Marlow, which we followed through Bourne End and Cookham.

Journey's end was now almost in sight as we left the mighty river and headed out over the Buckinghamshire heathland and forward via The Beeches Way to the village of Iver and home to the famous Pinewood Studios with its James Bond franchise.

We were now on the western outskirts of London and after arriving in Brentford, where we had another of our night stop-overs, we were again united with our old friend, Father Thames, and followed the river all the way into the heart of London.

The Embankment seemed to be busier than normal as the capital was building up towards the 2012 Olympics and under Tower Bridge were suspended giant versions of the trademark five rings.

Finally we reached journey's end at the Globe Theatre, where, when staff were told we had just finished Shakespeare's Way, we were given a private tour of this beautiful half-timbered building with its galleried interior.

Guide book: Shakespeare's Way published by The Shakespeare's Way Association - www.shakespearesway.org/

WALKING WITH WILLIAM

From birthplace up in Stratford
They walked the Shakespeare's Way
To Globe in far-off London
Where crowds would greet each play
Through villages that knew the Bard
Their footsteps forged ahead
Past cottage thatched in hamlets
And swathes of poppy red
Lonely country churches
With tombs ornate inside
Yet beneath a simple stone
Lay Winston and his bride
Along the Thames at Marlow
Then on to join the lines
That thronged along its city banks
Beneath Olympic signs
We'll never know if William
Strode upon these routes
But they enjoyed the journey
With packs and sturdy boots.

THE SOUTHERN C0AST TO COAST
Weston-super-Mare to Dover – 283 miles

Landmarks can be very frustrating because they often take literally hours and hours to disappear from view, if you are a cross country walker, and make one feel like a snail crossing an OS map.

And so it was the day after Peter and I set out to follow the coast-to-coast route and Somerset's mighty Mendip Hills transmitter came into our skyline view.

But surely, readers might point out, the 192-miles coast-to-coast walk runs from St Bees, Cumbria, across the Lake District, the Pennines, and the North York Moors to Robin Hood's Bay.

Yes, this is true, but we were following the alternative coast-to-coast path across Southern England from Weston-super-Mare on the Bristol Channel coast to Dover and the English Channel.

Ahead of us lay a wonderful trek across magnificent country, packed with sights of interest, through quiet water meadows and ancient woodland, traversing limestone and chalk downs and encountering many picturesque villages and bustling market towns along the way.

But all that lay in the future as we trudged to the top of the first of many hill ranges and saw the pencil-slim Mendip Transmitter in the distance ahead of us.

We were now following the West Mendip Way from Weston-super-Mare to the medieval city of Wells with its magnificent cathedral, built between 1175 and 1490, and here we picked up the East Mendip Way to guide us across the hills to Shepton Mallet.

And it was only when that 293-metre-high transmitter finally slipped below the horizon on a golden autumn afternoon that we truly felt we were on our way.

Just outside Shepton Mallet, we stopped beside some cottages at the edge of a field and were pondering the way to go when up popped a villager, who had been gardening behind a wall, and pointed out our route.

143

It was the first of many small kindnesses shown to these gentlemen of the road by those we happened to meet along the way.

A day's walking through gentle rolling Somerset countryside into Wiltshire brought us to the Army town of Warminster and from there we skirted the southern edge of Salisbury Plain, by way of a series of prehistoric hill forts, to drop down and stay in the village of Heytesbury at the end of the tranquil Wylye Valley.

Then followed a wonderful day's stroll through quiet meadows beside the River Wylye and far from the madding crowd - namely the busy main road linking Warminster with Salisbury on the hillside above us.

The following morning we were sitting outside St Mary's Church in the small village of Wylye enjoying a coffee when we fell into conversation with a local lady.

She told us the story of an impoverished village Jack the Lad, who went off to seek and make his fortune.

Apparently, on returning in a coach-and-four and finding his mother and sister in pauper's graves, he ordered the local stone mason to build them a fine tomb, but then went off to the Napoleonic wars without paying!

We were now on the Imber Trail, which neatly links the East Mendip Way with Salisbury, and stopped for the night in Wilton, a small town of rich heritage dating back to Saxon times and where carpets have been made since the 18th century.

From here it was a short walk into Salisbury and we jostled with crowds of tourists wandering through its ancient streets and clustering around its 11th Century cathedral like bees around a honey pot.

It was all a little disconcerting, but only served to enhance the sense of peace which followed, as we strolled away from the city through quiet water meadows.

We had now reached an important milestone as we were beginning the Clarendon Way, which passes from Wiltshire into Hampshire and runs for 25 miles over the low hills of the Test Valley to link with Winchester and its ancient cathedral.

We have often walked across open and featureless common land, where finding the way can be confusing and on this particularly cold winter's day, we'd stopped and were puzzling over the map, when a group of Hash Harriers came running towards us.

These are an international group of non-competitive running social clubs, humorously known as 'a drinking club with a running problem', where a 'hare' leaves a trail of paper, flour or chalk to be followed by the 'pack' or 'hounds'.

To our surprise, they stopped because these 'hounds' had just spotted some beer, left as a surprise by the 'hare' they'd been chasing, and their leader, a Major Justin Case (sic) offered us a can.

They were all pretty hot from the chase, so an ice-cold beer was just what they wanted, but we were cold from standing around and a warming coffee from our flasks would have been far more welcome

But it would have been churlish to decline, so we graciously accepted and surprisingly that beer tasted remarkably good.

The major pointed out our route before he and his merry men, now refreshed, went running off in pursuit of their hare, but was his title really Major Justin Case, we wondered.

Another two glorious sunny winter days walking along quiet lanes, through undulating countryside dotted with woodland and small villages, brought us out in a clearing above Winchester and we paused to check our map.

A family wandered into view clutching a single sheet map of a local walk and were obviously lost.

"Excuse me, but can you tell us where we are?" asked the mum. "Yes, you're in Hampshire," Peter replied. "But don't worry, I'm sure we can help," he quickly added.

Winchester Cathedral – Getty Images

After exploring Winchester, visiting the magnificent cathedral and staying overnight, it was time to hit the trail again and we picked up the River Itchen, east of the city, and followed it to the watercress beds at Alresford and the famous Watercress Line

As the light was beginning to fade, we dropped down through woodland into Selborne set within the northern boundary of the South Downs National Park.

This attractive village, amid the trees, is famous for its association with the 18th Century literary naturalist Gilbert White, whose book, The Natural History of Selborne, records his observations on local animals, birds and plant life, and has been continuously in print since 1789.

After an evening meal at the lively Selborne Arms, where preparations were in hand for a Hawaiian Night, and a comfortable night's B&B stay, we emerged into a snow-white world and regained the path as it led through St Mary's churchyard.

Here, to our delight, we spotted the tell-tale tracks of a roving fox.

The way now led us to picturesque Hazelmere and the start of the Greensand Way, which runs for 108 miles across the Surrey Hills and on into Kent, the Garden of England.

The footpath gains its name from its layers of sandstone, containing the green mineral, glauconite, and its greenish and sandy-coloured surface can be extremely slippery when wet, as we found to our cost on more than one occasion on this undulating route

We were also surprised to find just how wooded Kent was and that we were able to walk for miles through orchards without meeting a soul.

It was on this section that we passed through the Chartwell Estate, home to Sir Winston Churchill from 1922 until his death in 1965.

And it was here that I fell into a deep ditch. hidden by long grass and ended up tortoise-like on my back with my rucksack underneath me. Thank goodness there was no water in it!

It was also on this section that we got soaked in a sudden downpour and fled to the shelter of a nearby railway station to put on dry clothes. Peter said it gave a whole new meaning to the phrase: "Change at Pluckley."

We caught our first glimpse of the sea on a chalk escarpment at Aldington and followed the Saxon Shore Way through Hythe, Sandgate and Folkestone and along the top of those famous white cliffs, passing its moving memorial to 'The Few,' and so on to Dover

But my abiding memory of those last 70 miles was passing two small boys in a country lane one evening.

"Where are you going, mister?" one asked. "All the way to Dover," we replied. There was a pause. "Yer joking, aint yer, mister?"

Guide book: Cicerone Guides' Southern Coast-to Coast Walk, Weston-super-Mare to Dover by Ray Quinlan - www.cicerone.co.uk/

SNOWFALL IN SELBORNE

While late-night revellers lie abed
The walkers are abroad
Setting out upon their way
With evening memories stored
The valley village silent
Mantled now with snow
And just a friendly parson
To watch them as they go

A hush upon the churchyard
No wind to make a sound
Just trace of where a roaming fox
Has rested on the ground
Such visual signs of wildlife
Recorded by one wise -
Gilbert White the naturalist,
Who opened others' eyes
The Zig Zag path with brother carved
Still steep descends the hill
It's lasted over centuries past
And guides one's footsteps still.

SCARPA BOOTS

From moorland hills to country lanes
On paths and way-marked routes
For walking in all weathers
I love my Scarpa boots
Rugged and dependable
No matter the terrain
Comfortable and durable
Impervious to rain
I've criss-crossed Britain several times
To hiking trails complete
I've gear to keep me warm and dry
But Scarpa guards my feet.

THE STAFFORDSHIRE & WORCESTERSHIRE CANAL

Great Haywood to Stourport-on-Severn – 46 miles

It was another déjà vu moment as we stood at the Great Haywood Junction of the Trent & Mersey Canal on a freezing cold January morning.

Peter and I vividly recalled the glorious summer afternoon we had sat on a seat eating ice cream, while brightly-painted narrowboats puttered past and crowds of folk were everywhere enjoying the sunshine.

Now without a soul in sight, we were setting out to walk from this junction down the Staffordshire & Worcestershire Canal to Stourport-on-Severn.

This delightfully-rural waterway, opened in 1777 to carry goods from the Potteries west to Gloucester and onward down the River Severn to the bustling seaport and city of Bristol, was the latest piece in the jigsaw of canal walks, which we had been completing over the past twenty years.

The sky was ominously overcast and the towpath muddy and slippery as we started trudging the first eleven miles to our overnight stop in the small market town of Penkridge.

We had not gone far when we came upon a cluster of early primroses together with a small wooden plaque placed there by a group of locals giving thanks for surviving the Covid epidemic.

While bare-branched trees cast skeletal reflections over the still waters, the distinctive cries of wild geese came drifting over on the still air from nearby water meadows and the now waterlogged flood plains of the River Sow.

It was an early disappointment that this canal had no distinctive metal markers to help us count down the miles to our day's journeys end. But by way of a small compensation, all its lovely old stone bridges were individually named instead of simply numbered and this we had not seen before.

We were also interested to find that many of the old metal strips used at the end of the bridges to protect the stonework from the horse-drawn barge towing ropes were still there, together with the grooves that had been made in them over the years.

By early afternoon the BBC weather girl's forecast sun put in a late appearance, but was low in the sky and also reflecting off the water, which made picking our way along the slippery towpath directly into its blinding light particularly difficult.

Six hours of walking all through open country and with only two passing narrowboats and a handful of dog walkers for company, brought us at last to Penkridge and a warm welcome at The Littleton Arms, a Grade Two-listed 18th Century coaching inn, where we were booked in for the night.

Regaining the canal early the following morning, there was now an icy golden sheen on the water as we crunched along the frozen towpath, but, hang on a minute - why was the rising sun still shining directly into our eyes?

Then the penny dropped because the previous afternoon, and without our noticing it, the towpath had swung around from West to East before correcting itself a mile or so further on.

By coffee time we had reached Gailey Lock and the 340-foot summit of the Staffordshire and Worcestershire Canal, having now climbed 150 feet from Great Haywood Junction and here, overlooking the top lock, we came upon a magnificent roundhouse dating back to the year of Trafalgar.

It is thought to have been inspired by the Martello Towers built as a defensive measure during the Napoleonic Wars.

Again we had this peaceful rural landscape under clear blue winter skies entirely to ourselves, until we came upon a most welcome sight, namely The Anchor Inn at Cross Green, on the outskirts of Wolverhampton where 'muddy boots were welcome'.

The sandwiches we had bought earlier would now have to wait until tomorrow, we decided, before entering for lunch.

Back on the canal, we continued walking for an hour or so before diverting via a lane and a series of busy roundabouts to reach our Premier Inn at Wolverhampton North.

The prospect of risking life and limb by attempting to retrace our steps in the morning rush hour was not a good idea, so we booked a taxi to take us on to the next canal bridge.

But it snowed heavily overnight, which inevitably delayed our departure, and when at last we reached our drop-off point there was no canal to be seen!

Luckily a local called Roger was able to point out the right direction and we were soon back on course and following a surprisingly-rural way out of the city along a linear park under now clear blue skies with a dazzling white towpath underfoot.

Passing junctions with the Shropshire Union, a completed piece in our jigsaw, and the Birmingham canals, we were quickly out into open and sometimes wooded country amid low hills.

Just above Compton Lock, we came upon the first of a series of distinctive stone-built and circular Lobsterpot Weirs designed by famous Victorian canal builder and engineer James Brindley to prevent tree branches and other debris entering his water channels.

We picnicked against a sunny wall before setting out on our afternoon walk to Wombourne and here on leaving the canal, we faced a 1.7-mile tramp up a busy main road, but luckily help was at hand with the appearance of a waggon and horses.

It was, of course, an inn of that name and five minutes later, we were enjoying a rest and a drink and waiting for a local taxi driver to take us to the 17th century Himley House Hotel and then back to the path in the morning.

Our final day on the walk was to prove to be the most scenic of all and we'd not gone far when we came upon 'fisherman' Andy Timmins from Dudley beside a lock. But he was using a hand-held line with magnet on the end and was not at all interested in fish.

He had recently recovered three Roman coins. but sadly, they had turned out to be fake.

The canal now began forging its way between low and wooded hills, along a series of shallow valleys and through patches of quiet woodland until we arrived in the village of Kinver and The Vine Inn for lunch.

That afternoon the canal led us through more delightful countryside into Worcestershire and beyond to Kidderminster where we were treated to a magnificent late afternoon waterside view of the town's Grade One listed St Mary and All Saints parish church.

We stayed overnight at another nearby Premier Inn before setting out on the final three-miles walk into Stourport on Severn,

The rising sun, casting a golden glow over the water and setting the bordering bracken ablaze as the canal wound its way around a wooded hillside, was spectacular and made a fitting finale to our latest adventure.

Guide book: J.M Pearson's Canal Companion: Stourport & Black Country Rings/Birmingham Canal Navigations - www.jmpearson.co.uk/

TOWPATH IN WINTER

Winter towpath walking
Geese skeins call overhead
Muddy sections underfoot
Careful where you tread
Slate grey the skies reflection
In meadows turned to lakes
Bare tree in midst of wildfowl
The mirrored surface breaks
A lock beside a cottage
For narrowboats awaits
But with a lack of traffic
Fast closed remain its gates

Up ahead a lone craft
Disturbs the waters calm
Chugging onward steadily
As coots scoot out of harm
Beneath the brick bridge arches
Deep grooves in iron posts
Carved by horse-drawn barges
Now watched by boatmen's ghosts.
Yellow-green the branches
Strewn across the track
Cast down from treetops up above
By gale force winds attack
Locks and bridges punctuation
Marking stages on the walk
Unusual names on metal plaques
Prompting an impromptu talk
Smoke from out the chimney stack
Of lonely moored-up boat
Ice upon the waters
Where mallards quietly float
Near the rushing M6
A waterfall of sound
Path mud now lies frost-hardened
And not a soul around
Then overnight came snowfall
The world transformed to white
Hidden now the pathway
Grass verges out of sight
Each twig all clothed in icing
That edged the leaves of green
A sky that turned dawn rosy
Above the wintry scene
Heron in the sunlight
Pale spectre greets the day
Rising up above canal
On wide wings borne away

Another night of temperatures
Heading down so low
The waters now left hardened
By bank to bank ice floe
Inlaid upon the whiteness
Dog walkers leave a trail
Prints of boots and active paws
To tell a winter's tale

THE STRATFORD CANAL
Birmingham to Stratford-upon-Avon – 25 miles

The walkers now departing from Platform Two on the railway station close to the famous Cadbury World chocolate factory were not heading by train into Birmingham, but out of a convenient side gate and by foot along the canal towpath to historic Stratford-upon-Avon!

But first, early on that cold and grey January morning, Peter and I, had a brisk twenty-minute stride along the Birmingham and Worcester canal to its leafy Kings Norton junction with the Stratford canal.

This waterway with its 56 locks lowering the canal some three hundred feet on its passage to Stratford was constructed between 1793 and 1816.

Its original purpose was for the transportation of coal from the River Severn to Birmingham, but today it is a magnet for thousands of narrowboat enthusiasts being drawn towards Shakespearean Stratford.

Walking England's amazing network of canals is always full of surprises and this day was no exception when we suddenly came across a Guillotine Lock, the first we had ever seen.

Its purpose, we were told, was to maintain the water level between the two waterways, but the truth, according to a local lady, who happened to be passing by, was to stop the Birmingham and Worcester canal owners pinching water from their rivals, who operated the Stratford waterway.

Now we were approaching the deep wooded cutting leading to the 322-metre long Brandwood Tunnel - wide enough for two narrowboats to pass, but with no towpath for walkers.

In former times, barges were pulled through by hand via a rail set in the brick lining of the tunnel, while their horses were led over the top.

So, using Shanks's Pony, we emerged into suburbia with absolutely no sign of that long-obliterated horse track of old and even a local dog walker didn't have a clue as to which way we should go!

But following roughly along the line of the tunnel to a junction of roads, we crossed over and then noticed a footpath leading down an incline beside a row of houses and, yes, we had found the remains of that long-lost track!

Why the local council had never thought to provide what must be many thousands of walkers with a few simple direction signs, we could not imagine.

We began making our way gradually out into open country, but not before we received an urban shock from what was billed as a village for the 21st century at Dickens Heath, namely a huge apartments complex, together with a mock waterfall tumbling towards the canal.

Not long afterwards, we left the canal at Bridge 19 for lunch at the nearby Blue Bell Inn before crossing under the busy M42 and later diverting onto a lane to walk into Hockley Heath, where we were booked in at a Premier Inn.

Early the following morning, we walked back into the village centre to pick up sandwiches from the Co-op, but then walked around in a circle trying to find our way back onto the towpath, only to discover it was a few steps away, via a pub car park.

With some thirteen miles to go to our next overnight stop and having already wasted some precious time, we picked up the pace to escape from the West Midlands into Warwickshire and were soon approaching the Lapworth flight of twenty-five locks all within two miles.

Every so often we had spotted small metal posts marking the distance travelled from Kings Norton Junction and, installed by the Stratford-upon-Avon Canal Society, founded in 1953 to completely restore and reopen all of the navigation from Lapworth to Stratford.

The completion of this huge task was celebrated in 1964 when the Queen Mother performed the reopening ceremony.

It was here at the Lapworth flight we noticed that all the canal bridges had a slit down the middle, which we were told, was to accommodate the ropes needed back in the days when horses provided all the barge pulling power.

Shortly afterwards, we reached the Kingswood Junction with a linking arm of the mighty Grand Union Canal, which we'd followed for 137 miles all the way from London to Birmingham on an earlier winter walking adventure.

It was while walking on through open country that we chanced upon a group of Solihull Ramblers Club members, so naturally we stopped for a chat and an impromptu photo call.

Talking to the people we meet along the way is all part of the enjoyment on our cross-country treks.

Meanwhile, another unusual feature of this particular canal walk, was the distinctive white painted barrel roof cottages, where the canal builders had used the same wooden frames as they had for the small canal bridges.

Now the so far quite restricted views began to open up as the canal shrugged off the last vestiges of the old Forest of Arden to emerge into the Alne Valley with journey's end in sight, some six miles ahead beyond the spectacular 158-yard-long iron Bearley Aqueduct.

We stayed the night in the village of Wilmcote, now a destination for Stratford sight-seeing coaches, because it was here that Shakespeare's mother, Mary Arden, had a farm.

Unfortunately, our hosts at the inn, named after the famous lady, were not serving food at the time, but they were more than happy for us to order a takeaway and have our supper in the bar.

Leaving just as it was getting light. we completed the last three miles into Stratford in time for breakfast.

Guide book: J.M Pearson's Canal Companion: South Midlands - www.jmpearson.co.uk/

STRIDING TO STRATFORD

Past the Bournville purple
Home of chocolate bars
Up to join a towpath
And leave the world of cars
From a station platform
With sign to guide their feet
To Kings Norton junction
Where two canals do meet
Ahead the town of Stratford
With many locks between
As grimy urban landscape
Gave way to scenes of green.

THE TEST WAY
Inkpen Beacon to Eling – 44 miles

What a fabulous trail is Hampshire's Test Way, which starts high on Inkpen Beacon, next to a hangman's gibbet, and not that far from Highclere Castle, made famous by the TV series, Downton Abbey.

Oh, how often my wife, Jenny, and I had sped down the busy A34 en route to Portsmouth and the ferry taking us to our second home in France, with absolutely no idea of just what we were missing only a stone's throw away.

Now Peter and I were setting out on our first eleven-mile walk through the rolling North Wessex Downs to the picturesque village of St Mary Bourne, which could easily have been the setting for an Agatha Christie Miss Marple mystery.

We came across delightful hamlets with centuries-old churches, thatched cottages and houses built of distinctive flint or red brick all along this lovely rural way.

On an impulse that perfect August morning we stopped at a cottage door displaying a Hampshire Open Studios sign in the village of Linkenholt and stepped inside to meet a local artist, Suzie Masser-King, who presented me with an amazing coincidence.

For there on her easel was a sandy beach scene, just around the corner from the Karma Hotel on St Martin's in the Isles of Scilly, some twenty-eight miles beyond Land's End, where Jenny and I had stayed only a few weeks earlier.

It turned out that the Scillies were also one of her favourite holiday haunts.

We picnicked above Ibthorpe and walked down into the tiny hamlet to find a thatcher hard at work with the help of his son.

He had carried out his ancient craft in and around the Bourne Valley all his working life and was now re-thatching cottages and houses that he worked on over twenty years ago, he told us.

We reached The George in St Mary Bourne after a walk over wooded hills and enjoyed a pint sat outside in the late afternoon sunshine.

This excellent inn, with rooms, had recently re-opened after a £250,000 refurbishment, and leaving it the following morning, the way led us past a large fishing lake, created by a local benefactor as a haven for wildlife.

Climbing the lane opposite, we chanced upon a tiny field mouse sitting on the verge, who kindly allowed me to take its picture.

Our next lane encounter was with a local delivery driver, who worked four days a week and spent the other three walking for miles around the local highways and byways with his dog, often stopping to chat with Test Way walkers.

Our walks allow us close encounters with wildlife and the Test Way was no exception – the path often crossed by scurrying pheasants.

But it was sad to see the pens, where the young birds were being fattened in preparation for the shooting season.

After a morning making our way ever onward through rolling and often wooded countryside, beside huge wheat fields and under giant skies, we arrived in the small village of Longparish and picnicked in the St Nicholas churchyard close to a small tributary of the River Test.

But the river was very much in evidence later when we dropped down into the village of Wherwell and crossed a long wooden footbridge over the quiet waters.

Here we came upon a delightful scene of local families having fun around a series of pools, set amid open grassy grounds in the late afternoon.

Now we were on the last four miles of our 13.5-mile walk along the river valley into the small town of Stockbridge with its wide and picturesque High Street.

And here our imaginary and fairly constant companion, the Cosmic Joker, chose to play a cruel trick on two by now quite weary walkers.

We were overnighting at The White Hart, which we knew was in the High Street, but we failed to spot it set back behind a large tree-covered roundabout at the top of the town, and so walked all the way to the bottom of the road before a friendly local pointed out our mistake.

The following morning, we rejoined the old railway track bed we had followed on the last leg of our walk into town and soon came upon a very old friend.

For a couple of miles further on we reached the point where the Test Way crosses the 26-mile-long Clarendon Way, between Salisbury and Winchester, which we had followed over thirty years before on our epic cross-country walk from Weston-super-Mare to Dover.

A short while later we branched off to cross the River Test and to walk via meadows and quiet lanes to the tiny hamlet of Mottisfont, where we picnicked in the grounds of the 12th Century St Andrew's Church.

Now followed quite a long afternoon spotting Test Way arrows and weaving our way through patches of tangled woodland, through stubble-gold open country and along overgrown field paths, until we came at last to our overnight stop in the historic market town of Romsey with its many fine period buildings.

Here we stayed overnight at the comfortable Palmerston Rooms. named after the famous 19th Century politician, Lord Palmerston, whose impressive statue has pride of place in the town centre,

Early the following morning, we made our way back to the 16th Century Sadler's Mill, from whence we'd entered the town, and after a short walk along a busy main road, we were back in open country with Broadlands, the landmark Palladian mansion and home of the Mountbatten family, soon coming into view,

The River Test is one of the finest of only two hundred chalk streams in the world and was very much in evidence on our nine-mile trek to journey's end at Eling Wharf on the Solent.

One final highlight was the long board walk, snaking its way through the wild and marshy Lower Test Nature Reserve.

Guide book: Cicerone Guides' Walking Hampshire's Test Way - www.cicerone.co.uk/

PASSING THE TEST

Through fields of corn full ripened
As summer hours flow by
Above the red kites wheeling
Against the cloud-flecked sky
Sweeping views across the downs
From green hill's wooded crest
Then dropping down through shady lanes
To reach the River Test
A wood bridge crossing over
A track that gently follows
To where the village children
Play gaily in the shallows
Of Hampshire's finest waterway
Where salmon come to spawn
In waters clear as crystal
And new life here is born.

FEEDING AN ILLUSION

Pheasants on the farm track
Pheasants in the fields
Scattering 'cross the brown earth
As walkers are revealed
Up above a buzzard
Sends its piercing call
Drifting high on outswept wings
With eyes that see it all
Green feeders lure the lean brown birds
To take their fill of seed
Unmindful that this kindness
Just helps the shooters' need
Within a cage of wood and wire
Ignorant of their fate
The young so sadly unaware
That serried guns await.

THE THAMES PATH
Woolwich to Kemble – 185 miles

It was a magnificent September dawn just before the ' Great Fire of London' when Peter and I joined the mighty River Thames just upstream from its iconic barrier.

No, we were not time travellers in a muddle.

We just happened to be setting out on the Thames Path walk to the river's source in Gloucestershire, as the final preparations were being made to set alight a floating replica of 17th century London to commemorate the 350th anniversary of the great conflagration.

Starting a long-distance walk at 6am has definite advantages in summer, because one can cover three or four miles before breakfast and, because it was the Thames, we felt sure we'd find a convenient café along the way.

Sunrise came a few minutes later, illuminating the giant sand wharf gantry, where aggregates from the English Channel were being discharged by the Tarmac Marine's dredgers, City of London and City of Westminster.

I was thrilled to think that this working link with river and sea was helping to fuel London's building boom, many dramatic examples of which we were to see and indeed experience through temporary path diversions along the way.

'Path ahead closed' a notice told us on approaching a flashy riverside apartments building site, but, because someone had written 'really' below the sign, we assumed the way was actually still open and carried on.

We were wrong and having wasted many a step vowed that in future we'd faithfully follow all marked diversions.

Soon I had taken off my waterproof, donned because there was a nip in the air, and had rolled up my walking trousers to just above the knees, but had kept on my trustee Tilley Hat.

We'd been walking for about an hour when we came upon a couple in white robes enjoying takeaway cups of coffee beside a high wire fence, beyond which was a new hotel.

Peter walked up to them and asked "Do you want help escaping?"

The woman probably in her early twenties with long flowing black hair and drop-dead-gorgeous, just looked at these two elderly gents in their crumpled walking shorts, shirts and hats, and quick as a flash replied: "Why have they let you two out for the day?"

We roared with laughter. Yes, we'd been let out, not just for one day but for three whole days, while we walked the first 48 miles from Woolwich to Staines, leaving my wife, Jenny, at home working in our cottage garden.

We walked on past the Millennium Dome and soon reached the famous Cutty Sark sailing ship and deciding it was time for breakfast, we turned our back on the river and quickly found a bakery and coffee shop.

Luckily the Thames Path National Trail is well marked, so after breakfast all we had to do was follow it faithfully, but suddenly our way was blocked by a pair of locked gates!

We had reached the Surrey Docks Community Farm, one of five around the city, and a notice told us the gates would be open at 10 am, but would they?

It was 9.45am, so we called the number provided and luckily the manager came to let us in and told us how right up until the 1930s people suffering from smallpox had been put aboard a ship moored there and taken by river out of the city to recover in isolation.

By noon we were at Tower Bridge and walked on through crowds of tourists to pass the Globe Theatre, the finishing point of our Shakespeare Way walk many years before.

On the opposite bank we could see the giant pontoon carrying the soon-to-be ignited replica of 17th century London.

Beyond the London Eye and Westminster Bridge, the Embankment path is awash with shoals of concrete and glass apartments, beyond which we detoured around the giant building site, which is the old Battersea Power Station, to reach our first night's hotel.

Again, we were away at dawn and walking through Battersea Park and back to the river, which we followed until hunger drove us inland at Kew to find a café, where I had probably the best bacon bap I have ever tasted.

Being a Saturday morning, teams of rowers were out on the river, as we walked past Kew Gardens and on towards picturesque Richmond for lunch with the noise of jets coming in to land at Heathrow now making their presence rudely felt.

While swans, geese and dabbling ducks kept us company for much of the way that day, the high-pitched cries of parakeets filled the skies and so endemic have these tenacious immigrants become that one had even found its way onto a pub sign.

By now the Thames had become a quiet meandering river tamed by locks and it all seemed a far cry from the hustle and bustle of the capital city.

We reached Kingston-on-Thames around teatime and crossed the river to our hotel for the night.

Our luck held and it was another wonderful dawn as we regained the path for our final fifteen-mile walk to Staines via Hampton Court, reaching Henry the Eighth's lavish palace around 7.30am.

But now it seemed there was a ferry crossing between us and journey's end and what if it was not running?

Luckily our guide book contained a telephone number and the ferryman, who operates a year-round service, confirmed he would be there to meet us when we reached Shepperton Lock.

The sandwiches we bought at the cafe by the roundabout in East Molesey were so full of salmon that we only had room for one on our walk into Staines and that was to prove a stroke of luck.

Had we tarried just another few minutes over lunch then, we would never have caught a late-running train that allowed us to get back to the West Country in record time.

The Thames Path – Staines to Pangbourne

We were welcomed by a rose-tinted dawn as we set out on the second stage of our Thames Path adventure and soon arrived at Runnymede water meadow.

It was here that King John signed that famous charter in 1215 and while the early light added great atmosphere to the scene, I cursed that it was no good for pictures, at least not on a mobile phone.

We were now en route for Windsor and had passed Honeypot Cottage on the far bank, where the late actress, Beryl Reid, once lived with her thirteen cats, when we suddenly popped out on the busy main road into Datchet.

It was 8am and as we trudged along keeping pace with the commuter traffic, our thoughts turned to breakfast. Might we find some in this small Berkshire town, I wondered?

This' will we or won't we be lucky' situation always adds a little extra spice to our adventures.

Yes, we were in luck and were soon munching bacon and egg baps in a cafe run by a young lady, who didn't seem to mind that these two early customers had completely taken over her small dining space, with their large backpacks, walking poles and other paraphernalia.

Not long after regaining the path I happened to glance towards the river and was rewarded with a first glimpse of Windsor Castle popping up over the tree tops and not far away.

The trail now led through some wonderful open parkland with the castle appearing to melt into the far distance and I wondered what had become of Windsor.

Had I looked at our map, I would have seen that the Thames was looping around and before we knew it, we were walking into the bustling riverside heart of that historic town.

People were taking coffee in the sunshine at a bistro terrace opposite and we decided it would be churlish not to walk over the bridge and join them.

Not far beyond the town, we entered a massive concrete portal, above which traffic thundered over the river on the Windsor by-pass, and were treated to a huge mural of faces staring out at us through the gloom.

It had been painted under the Elizabeth Bridge by London artist Cosmo Sarson, ahead of the Olympic Games, a passerby told us. So, the New Yorker we had met walking the other way earlier, was certainly right, when he spoke of surprises.

He told us: "It's my fifth walking vacation in England and I saved this trail till last thinking it would be flat and dull, but I was wrong and it's turning out to be the best yet, because there has been so much of interest to see."

Making an early start meant that by lunchtime we could slow the pace and enjoy a sunny afternoon, strolling along past Eton and its college and later, on the far bank, Oakley Court, where the famous St Trinian's films were made, featuring its anarchic school for uncontrollable girls.

Approaching our stopover in Maidenhead, we passed under Brunel's railway bridge, which has the longest and flattest brick arches in the world, so much so that Victorians thought it would collapse under the weight of the first train en route from Bristol to Paddington.

We donned full waterproofs the following morning, ahead of a pending storm, and made our way back to the still-darkened river, luckily illuminated by nearby street lights.

The route to Marlow was refreshingly wild, but we had only been walking for an hour when the rain finally overtook us with a vengeance, so much so that we were wet and muddy on emerging into Marlow High Street around 9.45am and ready for a late breakfast.

We were made very welcome in a nearby cafe and bakery, despite our bedraggled appearance, and when we left an hour later the sun was shining.

The eight-mile walk on to famous Henley-on-Thames was delightful with time spent sitting beside picturesque Hurley Lock and chatting with passing boat skippers, while enjoying mugs of hot chocolate from a nearby cafe.

But the highlight was climbing away from the river and walking through the rolling parkland of the Culham Court Estate, enjoying fabulous views across the Thames Valley and with yet another surprise in store!

For there on the skyline was a new ultra-modern Roman Catholic Church, built recently by the Swiss financier, Urs Schwarzenbach, who had acquired the 650-acre estate.

After lunch at The Flower Pot Inn, which was stuffed with curios, we walked on to Henley, accompanied by the squawking of Canada geese and the sharp cries of instructors calling to rowers out on the water.

Another rosy dawn saw us on the trail en route for Sonning, where, according to a dog walker we met, a hearty breakfast was to be found at The Great House.

"You know, Pete, the only thing this trail lacks are distance markers," I said.

The words were literally just out of my mouth, when we came upon a fingerpost telling us that Sonning and breakfast were only three miles ahead.

I was not particularly looking forward to walking through Reading on our way to journey's end at Pangbourne railway station, but as it turned out, the town has made much of its riverside amenity, so that was the final surprise.

The Thames Path – Pangbourne to Abingdon

Winston Churchill once said history was comprised of the lives of famous people and that thought crossed my mind as Peter and I set out from Pangbourne-on-Thames on a chilly March morning to continue our trek along England's most famous river.

For our trusty guide book told us we were to encounter memories of those great writers, Kenneth Grahame and HG Wells, but we had no idea we were also to come across a sad reminder of much-loved singing superstar George Michael.

It was shortly after crossing the Thames that we passed Pangbourne Parish Church and the cottage, where Wind in the Willows author Kenneth Grahame lived from 1924.

And it was as a moving tribute to him that fresh willows were cut from the river to decorate the church for his funeral in 1932.

The way out of the town climbs up a road lined with lovely old houses before turning along a lane leading to a footpath, which trends across open and wooded hillsides commanding views over the Thames.

But it was after descending to the river that the first of the day's surprises was sprung on us as, with eyes front, we trudged passed an exercise paddock for horses.

I just happened to glance sideways to see myself, walking poles in hand, some thirty yards away and it was not until I had done a double-take that I realised I was looking into a large and very long mirror, I guess used for training purposes.

Naturally we couldn't resist taking reflected pictures of ourselves before moving off and quickly encountering surprise number two.

There, growing close to the abutments of a main-line railway bridge across the Thames, was a large Christmas tree still decorated with red baubles.

We hoped a passing dog walker might know why, but to no avail, although she alerted us to a very poignant and sadly-moving sight a little further along the way, which now led through open meadows with a fabulous backdrop of woodland beyond the meandering river.

For it was on entering the pretty village of Goring-on-Thames that we passed the riverside home of singing super star George Michael, who had died on Christmas Day, 2016, and was revealed to have done a considerable amount for charity in his own quiet way.

Such was the loss felt by fans of all ages across the world, that hundreds of letters and other moving tributes were still to be seen outside his home.

While sitting in the churchyard for a coffee, the sun came out and a lady, who happened to be passing by, told us that George was often seen around the village and had been accepted as just another member of the community.

I rather hoped that the writer of the next Thames Path guide would give him a worthy mention.

185

Having re-crossed the river, our way now led through a series of wide-open pastures with some magnificent properties dotted alongside the far bank.

Spring was in the air as we strolled along to the honking of Canada and greylag geese and with the haunting, whistling cries of kites circling in the skies overhead.

It was nearing noon and as we were approaching The Beetle and Wedge, our thoughts turned to a pre-lunch pint, where we now knew, thanks to our trusty guide book, that we would be in good literary company.

For it was when staying here that HG Wells wrote The History of Mr Polly, and while another famous guest was George Bernard Shaw, the riverside inn also featured in Jerome K Jerome's Three Men in a Boat.

The way now left the river and we were dragged reluctantly back to the 21st century for a twenty-minute slog along a busy road and over a main railway line before being allowed to escape into a quiet country lane and so back to the Thames.

Now the wide views had been replaced by much narrower vistas of tall waving reeds, willows and other trees, yet to turn green, and it was definitely time for lunch, so we took off our sacks, used them as back rests, and settled down for a break.

Again the 21st century reimposed itself with a ping as I received an update text from my wife Jenny, and Peter made a check call to a work colleague.

That afternoon, we walked into picturesque Wallingford and found a tea shop where we chatted to a young woman, who'd just moved to the town from Wales and had 'escaped' with her laptop to do some work while her partner continued the unpacking.

If she enjoyed long-distance walking, she could now follow the Thames to London or to the river's source in Gloucestershire, we told her.

And if she was feeling even more energetic, she could also follow The Greater Ridgeway from Wallingford to the South Coast at Lyme Regis in Dorset, or to the North Sea at Hunstanton in Norfolk, a walk we had done a decade before.

The sun, which had been flirting with us all day, now decided to stay out and we enjoyed a lovely early evening walk into the village of Benson, where, close to a spectacular weir bridge, we came upon a riverside terrace bar and could not resist a glass of chilled white wine.

But then we had to pay for it with a mile and a half yomp in the gathering gloom to reach our hotel at Shillingford, where having been told its bridge was one of the prettiest on the Thames, we rose to picture it at sunrise.

From there it was an eleven-mile stroll under clear blue skies through gloriously open countryside away from most habitation, as Old Father Thames made a series of long and gentle loops on the way to the historic market town of Abingdon - sadly, our journey's end on this occasion.

The Thames Path – Abingdon to the Source

There is something magical about leaving a town at dawn when most are still asleep and when many untrodden miles lie ahead.

And so it was when Peter and I left Abingdon, one of the oldest inhabited towns in England, at 5am on a glorious midsummer morning.

We were on the final stage of our trek along the River Thames from London's famous barrier to its slender source in rural Gloucestershire and tucked away in our rucksacks was breakfast to be had in some peaceful spot.

"I wonder what adventures we shall have today," I always ask and on this final journey we were to be richly rewarded by meeting a giant rabbit in human form and a famous jazz guitarist.

Beyond Abingdon is one of the more remote stretches of the now meandering Thames and we were soon passing through riverside grounds landscaped by Capability Brown as part of the nearby Nuneham Palladian villa.

Author Lewis Carroll organised river trips from Oxford to picnic here and stroll in the woods when the party included the original Alice.

And talking of picnics, our thoughts turned to breakfast as we strolled through winnowing meadow grasslands, where almost every step threw up a shower of tiny butterflies.

We found a spot for our trusty plastic sheet and out came bottles of freshly-squeezed orange juice, croissants, bananas and coffee.

It was only nine and half miles to Oxford, so this was a leisurely day to prepare us for the twenty-mile trek from city of dreaming spires towards Lechlade on the southern edge of The Cotswolds.

The Thames passes though the edge of Oxford and here we stopped at a riverside pub, aptly named The Punter, before leaving the river to do a little exploring around the neighbourhood.

After overnighting in a nearby hotel, we again left at 5am, crossed Osney Bridge, famed for having the lowest headroom on the river, and had the world to ourselves, until we heard laughter.

There in a large natural pool, sparkling gold in the early morning sunlight, three young people were enjoying a dip. "It's lovely and warm," they cried back in answer to Peter's shouted enquiry, but we didn't think we'd stop to find out, although, in hindsight, it might have been fun.

Ahead lay a glorious day of walking through long stretches of water meadow and fingers of woodland reaching out to touch the river, all interspersed by locks, beautifully maintained and garlanded with flowers.

While chicks and small warblers cheeped and chirped amid the rustling reeds, the whistling cries of both buzzards and kites was often heard in the ever-changing skies.

Because we'd made an early start, we covered the 13.5 miles to Newbridge in time for a pub lunch and what a treat it was to shed our heavy packs. Ironically the bridge built by French Benedictines around 1250 is one of the oldest on the Thames.

Ahead lay six miles to our stopping point at Tadpole Bridge, marred only by the final few, where the path was badly overgrown, but all was well the following morning as we enjoyed another lovely day's walking on to our overnight pub stop in historic Lechlade.

Here we awoke to rain-filled skies and donned waterproofs in preparation for a soaking, but what a memorable day it was to be.

We'd not gone far when we spied a weird personage loitering by a hedge and went to investigate what turned out to be the scarecrow-like image of a tall thin lady with a bunny's head.

There was something quite spooky about her we agreed as we continued on our way to eventually arrive dripping at The Red Lion in Castle Eaton, said to be the first inn on the Thames.

We received the warmest of welcomes from our host as we divested ourselves of packs and waterproofs, before ordering lunch and getting into conversation with a fellow traveller, who happened to be heading in the opposite direction.

"So, what do you do for a living?" Peter asked after we had been chatting for some while and discovering that he was on his first long distance walk.

And what a surprise it was to discover that our chance acquaintance was John Etheridge, a famous UK virtuoso on acoustic and electric guitar, who Peter had heard play live in a bistro in Witney, Oxfordshire, some fifteen years earlier.

The rain eased as we trudged into picturesque Cricklade, the first town on the upper reaches of the Thames, and headed for our second Red Lion of the day and final overnight stay.

Clear blue skies greeted us as we set out on the final 13.5 miles to the Thames source, but that became much longer when we missed the path and were led siren-like along the linking Thames and Severn Way for well over a mile before realising our mistake.

Later, we walked through North Meadow, one of the finest uncultivated ancient grasslands in Britain, which hosts Britain's largest population of the Snake's Head Fritillary, a beautiful and nationally-scarce flower, we learned.

Now the way led through the Cotswold Water Park, a series of lakes created from disused gravel pits and on through sleepy Somerford Keynes and Kemble to arrive at the source of the mighty Thames, marked by a simple stone set in undulating farmland.

"So now that's done, where are we going to walk next?" Peter asked.

Guide book: Cicerone Guides' The Thames Path from Source by Leigh Hatt - www.cicerone.co.uk/

It was on our Thames Path walk that a chance remark made by a taxi driver, who was picking us up from Tadpole Bridge, near Bampton, Oxfordshire, inspired Peter to write the following poem.

The man had lifted our rucksacks into his boot before driving us back to our most recent starting place and was obviously impressed when he realised how heavy they were, exclaiming: "You must be men of steel."

MEN OF STEEL

A taxi driver named them
With his approval seal
"If you can walk those many miles,
You must be Men of Steel"
Their packs that he found heavy
To them were no big deal
When hefted on their shoulders
For they are Men of Steel
They've munched on buns and croissants
Between each hearty meal
And they don't count the calories
For they are Men of Steel
They've sometimes suffered blisters
On ball of foot and heel
But that won't stop their rambling
For they are Men of Steel
They might meet rams and big bulls
But that won't make them squeal
They'll vault a fence quite sprightly
For they are men of steel.
When oozing mud confronts them
They stay on even keel
Two sticks make them sure-footed
For they are Men of Steel
At dawn they're up and booted
And quietly off they steal
The morn's not made for lazing
For they are Men of Steel

While some like malls and shopping
For them there's no appeal
In trudging down some High Street
For they are Men of Steel
They won't just dine on travel films
That's boredom reel to reel
And weather never stops them
For they are Men of Steel
They mean to keep on going
Not end in chairs on wheel
And who knows they might do so
For they are Men of Steel.

SEEKING THE SOURCE

From barrier down in London
To lonely country source
They walked the length of Father Thames
With book to guide their course
Through crowds upon Embankment
They passed the turning Eye
And famous city landmarks
Outlined against the sky

They followed then the path that led
Into the countryside
Bustle swapped for rural peace
As water flowed beside
To Runnymede where King John signed
The Magna Carta laws
This brush with history savoured
They moved on without pause
Windsor's royal castle
And Oxford's dreaming spires
Waymarks on a journey
That met their hearts' desires
And then the climb to Cotswold heights
Where part-hidden in a field
Unremarked by many
A river's birth revealed.

THE TRENT & MERSEY CANAL

Preston Brook to Shardlow – 93.5 miles

One of the most alluring aspects of walking around Britain's amazing heritage networks of canals and waterways is that one never quite knows what to expect around the next bend or what the day will unfold.

So, it was when Peter and I set out on the Trent & Mersey Canal just beyond its conflux with the Bridgewater Canal in Preston Brook, Cheshire.

We hadn't been walking many minutes early on that sunny morning when we came upon a canal-side free library, beside which was a notice offering eggs for sale laid by Happy Hens!

We've come across many sights on our wanderings along Britain's myriad of cross-country footpaths in the summer and along the canals in the winter, but this was a first.

Not long afterwards, we reached the first of the five tunnels along this waterway, built early in the 18th century to link the mighty rivers Trent and Mersey and to serve the new industrial revolution town of Stoke-on-Trent and The Potteries.

Tunnels can often be something of a challenge for walkers because finding the way over the top of them is not always easy, but on this occasion, it was simply a case of following two linking lanes.

The canal now hugged the shoulder of the River Weaver valley through a rolling landscape of farmland, studded with belts of deciduous woodland, and it was on this section that we came upon a couple aboard their retirement narrowboat.

He had been a motor mechanic for thirty years until a serious illness forced the couple to re-evaluate their lives.

"We decided that life was too short, so we sold up our home and bought the boat four years ago and have never looked back," his wife told us.

Now we diverted through the village of Barnton to avoid the Barnton Tunnel and came upon The Jam Butty Boy!

This unique wood carving was created as a reminder of just how hard it was for local families to save up for their first house in the 1950s, often surviving on bread and jam.

By mid-afternoon the canal had led us into the industrial town of Anderton, where we came upon one of the so-called 'Seven Wonders of the Waterways,' namely The Anderton Lift.

Dating from 1875, this ingenious invention was designed to overcome the fifty-foot disparity between the canal and the River Weaver by raising and lowering narrowboats in two water-filled caissons.

Corrosion eventually forced its closure in 1983, but it was reopened in 2002 thanks to £7 million of Heritage Lottery funding and now has its own visitors' centre.

More industrial heritage awaited when, later that afternoon we called in at The Salt Barge pub, which, dating from 1861, slaked the thirst of generations of workers from the nearby Lion salt mine.

We began our day with a 'first' and so it was to end that way when on learning that our nearby hotel for the night was not serving an evening meal, we ordered in a Chinese take-away.

The management kindly provided plates and laid a table in their small lounge bar and we used the top of a nearby radiator as an improvised hot plate for the tin foil food containers.

Regaining the canal, the following morning, we were soon passing the massive Tata Chemicals plant, not a particularly pretty sight, but even here stencilled figures on a foot bridge illustrated the area's salt mining heritage.

The walk now led through the peaceful valley of the River Dane and on to Middlewich, where all the canal-side pubs were closed, but luckily a nearby fish and chip shop was open, so we dined on sausage butties sitting in a park before walking on to the busy town of Sandbach for the night.

On the following morning's walk, we came upon 'Heartbreak Hill,' so named by boaters because there are twenty-six locks in a seven-mile stretch as the canal ascends 250ft from the Cheshire plain and into Staffordshire.

All but one of these locks were doubled in the 1830s, so ingeniously allowing one to work as a mini reservoir for the other, while at the same time increasing the canal's capacity for delivering fuel to feed the furnaces in the pottery-producing towns.

By lunchtime we'd reached the one-and-a half-mile-long Harecastle Tunnel, built by engineer Thomas Brindley and called the 'wonder of the age', but only to be later replaced by a larger one built by Thomas Telford.

The tunnel runs under Harecastle Hill between Kidsgrove and Tunstall and is certainly a formidable barrier for those on foot.

Luckily there's an easy route, up a road and over the top, through parkland and returning to the far end of the tunnel close to a busy roundabout beyond the giant JCB factory and so on into Stoke-on-Trent.

Eighteenth century folk might well have marvelled at the Anderton Lift and called this tunnel 'the wonder of the age.'

But just what would they have made of the Tata Chemical Works, the JCB plant and traffic thundering along the M6 close to a set of those double locks we'd passed this morning?

THE TRENT & MERSEY CANAL - PART TWO
Stoke-on-Trent to Shardlow

It was a glorious early June morning when Peter and I set out to walk the final 63 miles of the magnificent Trent & Mersey Canal from the historic Etruria Junction, with its industrial heritage museum in the heart of Stoke-on-Trent, all the way to Shardlow in Derbyshire.

It was here at Etruria that Josiah Wedgwood based his famous pottery to benefit from waterway transport.

The Trent & Mersey is largely rural in nature and it was not long after leaving Stoke and its constant droning of traffic that we made our way out into the quietude of open country en route for the small canal-side market town of Stone.

The towpath hedgerows were awash with snow white hawthorn and May blossom, while the still waters were a myriad of reflections and the fields opposite ablaze with yellow buttercups.

While duck busily dabbled, wary swans guarded their fluffy broods snuggled up and sunbathing at the water's edge, causing us walkers to tiptoe quietly by.

Every now and again, narrowboats hove into view and cheery waves were exchanged.

Oh, what a contrast this was to that bleak February Monday morning when we'd set out from Preston Brook on the first 35-mile section to Stoke.

The opening of the canal in 1777 connected the River Trent Navigation, near Shardlow, with the Bridgewater canal at Preston Brook to provide an inland waterway link with the major ports of Hull and Liverpool.

But back to this glorious June afternoon and walking along the canal with every mile marked with a distinctive cast iron post telling us the ever-changing distances between Preston Brook and Shardlow.

Many of them were removed during World War Two, but now all have been faithfully reproduced and replaced thanks to the canal's preservation society.

We left the waterway at Sandon and strolled up the lane to The Dog and Doublet, where we indulged ourselves with a cream tea in the courtyard and stayed overnight.

Back on the canal, a wonderful morning's walk along the wide and peaceful Trent Valley took us past the last surviving natural inland salt marsh in the British Isles.

Here the salt was harvested and locally-produced beef was salted, put into barrels, also made for the brewing industry, and carried along the canal to feed the Royal Navy.

Shortly after reaching Great Haywood Junction, which links the Trent & Mersey with Stourport-on-Severn, disaster struck as the canal had been fenced off for essential maintenance work.

After quick look at the map, we diverted into Great Haywood and back to the canal only to find to our dismay that it was still barred to us.

But fortunately help was at hand with the arrival of a narrowboat owner, who had discovered a tiny parallel path, which we followed him along and back to his boat moored just beyond the blockade.

He and his wife had been living on their boat for many years and were the first of a number of couples we met who just loved their roving lives.

The canal, now fringed with bright yellow flag iris, meandered its way on through open country with every bend revealing new vistas until we came at last to our overnight stop at the Premier Inn in Shugborough.

Day Three dawned with clear blue skies and after a couple hours we were again well out into open country when we came across a shady seat made from a long dead tree - a perfect coffee stop.

But unknown to us it was already occupied and the minute we'd cast off our heavy packs and taken our ease out buzzed a family of bees.

We stopped for ice creams at busy Fradley Junction with the Coventry Canal and mentally made a note of that for yet another canal walk, already featured in this book.

Here we met another couple who live on their narrowboat and use it as a floating shop for all their wonderful rope fenders and everything from cat toys and key rings which they make during the winter months.

From here the towpath led us through quiet water meadows, where a sole bittern boomed, until we joined the mighty River Trent for a few minutes before it went tumbling over a weir and we continued on until we diverted off the canal to walk into Barton-under-Needwood to our overnight stop at The Shoulder of Mutton.

"We've been here before and stayed here before!" I said to Peter as I suffered yet another of those déjà vu moments and sure enough, the penny quickly dropped, when we recalled our earlier stopover there on one of our Macmillan Way cross-England treks.

How could one possibly forget previously staying in a village you might ask? But when one considers this book covers some forty years of rambles criss-crossing the country, then I feel that we can be forgiven.

And I never stop counting my blessings for Britain's wonderful network of paths there for all to enjoy.

I never dreamt we might need ear defenders, but they would have been welcome the following morning when we rejoined the canal only to walk for quite some distance with the roar of the A38 on one side and a gravel works on the other.

We were now en route for the famous brewing town of Burton and the canal's character had subtly changed from a water colourist's idyll to that of a more open and semi-urban environment with the faint aroma of brewer's malt carried on the air.

The canal snaked its way through the edge of the town and then on an aqueduct over the River Dove to Willington, where we overnighted at The Dragon.

We returned to the canal at 7am for the final 11 miles through quiet countryside, never far from the Trent, to journey's end in Shardlow - known in its heyday as the Rural Rotterdam.

En route, we met a professional dog walker, who'd unknowingly dropped his mobile phone and if we hadn't deviated just a few steps in time from the very beginning of our walk on the Monday and then hadn't stopped to talk to him, he'd never have spotted it lying on the grass at his feet.

Guide book: J.M. Pearson's Canal Companion: Cheshire Ring and South Pennine Ring - www.jmpearson.co.uk/

WALKING THE TRENT AND MERSEY

White sprinkles on the towpath
Where hawthorn's brushed by breeze
Yellow iris lining
Canal beneath the trees
New life takes to water
Before the parents' gaze
Cygnets and downy goslings
Glide through the summer haze
Between the sturdy lock gates
Beside retaining wall
The brightly-painted narrowboats
Gently rise and fall
June walking the Trent-Mersey
With birdsong all around
Strolling 'midst such beauty
An inner peace is found.

THE AMTRAK RAIL JOURNEYS

In 2003 and 2004 Peter and I decided to pause our long-distance walking in Britain and just sit back and enjoy two mammoth train journeys across the United States on the magnificent Amtrak trains.

Both trips started at Chicago's historic Union Station after an overnight stop with Peter's cousin, Roderick, and his wife, Karen, who live in the suburb of Winnetka, immortalised by jazz drummer Gene Krupa in his classic, Big Noise From Winnetka.

The station is the third busiest in the United States and Amtrak's fourth busiest hub, handling some 140,000 passengers on an average weekday, and standing dwarfed in the middle of its Beaux-Arts splendour this was easy to believe.

One journey took us across the Rockies to San Francisco and the other to Los Angeles via San Antonio in Texas.

We were sustained on our travels by wine boxes, nibbles from crisps and peanuts to pretzels and a pack of cards, with which we played numerous games of rummy, also our chosen pastime at the end of a day's walking back in the UK.

Our version in which a wild card is changed every round and the winner of a game is decided when the other player is more than 50 points down proves that it is luck not skill that matters in the end and what goes around comes around.

In Los Angeles, as we waited for a taxi to take us to the airport for the flight home, we worked out that we had played 400 games as we traversed the country and had won 200 each.

Amtrak Vacations UK for complete rail holiday packages - www.amtrakvacations.co.uk/

AMTRAK ADVENTURE – NUMBER ONE
Chicago to San Francisco – 2,438 miles

RIDING THE CALIFORNIA ZEPHYR

"Do you want grits?" the steward asked Peter and I.

We were seated in the dining car of the famous California Zephyr, the passenger train that runs all the way across the USA from Chicago, on the shores of Lake Michigan, to San Francisco on the Pacific coast.

Ahead lay three unforgettable sight-seeing-filled days as our sleek double-stack train, with top-deck viewing car, coursed its way across the plains of Nebraska to Denver, over the Rockies, forward over the plains to the Sierra Nevada range and on through Reno and Sacramento to San Francisco

What on earth were 'grits' we both wondered, only to be told this was a savoury side dish made from corn, so we happily tried a portion.

Grits may no longer be served, but this fabulous Federally-funded Amtrak railway journey across seven states and three time zones should be on today's menu for anyone who loves long distance train travel.

And if you happen to enjoy chatting to people, then you'll have the perfect opportunity of meeting Americans from all walks of life, who will mostly be boarding and later leaving the train at intervals all along the way.

For they will be your chance breakfast, lunch, and dinner companions, unless you happen to occupy a whole table as a party of four.

Our 2,438-mile rail-road ride began in late afternoon at Chicago's Union Station, with its lofty marbled halls, and with us wandering uncertainly along the platform amid all the hustle and bustle looking for our carriage.

We eventually located it just a couple of cars along from the restaurant carriage, so that was a bit of luck.

We'd booked a cabin, complete with comfortable chairs facing a large picture window from which we'd be able to watch America go by and with two pull-down bunks and a small toilet and shower.

Among our luggage essentials were two wine boxes, large packets of crisps and other nibbles and, of course, our playing cards for beginning yet another rummy contest, but what were we to do about wine glasses, we wondered.

We could hardly sneak them out of the dining car, but luckily the answer was near at hand, because there was a complimentary water dispenser and plastic cups at the end of every carriage.

It was April and there were still patches of snow on the ground as we pulled out of Chicago and began gathering speed and I savoured that unmistakeable tinge of excitement at the prospect of all that was to follow over the next couple of days.

In the first few hours, we travelled from Illinois into Iowa and then over the famous Mississippi River towards the sunset. We were now back in our compartment and sipping wine from our plastic cups, as prairie barns, lonely diners, and nameless townships went flashing by.

While we slept, our Zephyr moved on through Omaha and then crossed the Nebraska line as we gained another state and lost an hour and, in the morning, we had to change our watches to Mountain Time.

We enjoyed more expansive views from the dining car over breakfast as the Zephyr forged steadily on across the plains under clear blue skies towards Denver, Colorado.

I was raised in the Western cowboy movie era, when the city with its marshalling yards was the destination for all the big cattle droves, so the very name Denver held a boyhood fascination for me.

Today this is the famous modern 'mile high' city of the plains, but if you wanted to leave the train for a couple of days, you'd find plenty of reminders of the Old West in the city's Larimer Square, which features landmark buildings of the 19th century.

We hopped off the train to stretch our legs for a few minutes, but then it was back onboard to enjoy perhaps the most spectacular day of the trip from the Zephyr's domed observation car.

For Denver is on the edge of the Rocky Mountains and we were soon winding our way ever upwards through a series of tunnels and open passes with stunning views over now snowy mountainous landscapes.

We paused in a siding amid the pines to let a freight train go rattling by before entering the six-mile Moffat Tunnel and then hurtling out into the blinding light.

Now our Zephyr stopped again and we found ourselves in the midst of a truly Alpine scene cloaked in sunlit snow amid the pines and it was if we had suddenly entered another silent world.

Soon we were passing down the lovely Fraser Canyon with hoof prints of deer on the snowy banks and then on to Granby, which is the gateway to yet another of America's national parks

Joining the famous Colorado River, we followed it as it contoured around the pine-clad Rockies, passing time and again over the fast-flowing river with its mini rapids and tiny pebble beaches.

The views from the Zephyr's observation car were spectacular and ever changing and it was rather like being lost in the midst of our own travel documentary.

Late afternoon brought us down to Glenwood Springs and more memories of the old West. For it was here that Doc Holliday, gambler, gunfighter, dentist and friend of Wyatt Earp, is buried. He survived the famous Gunfight at the OK Corral with a bullet graze, only do die in his bed of tuberculosis – his last words allegedly – "This is funny."

As I mentioned earlier, I grew up in the 1950s and early 1960s, the era of the Cowboy Westerns, which I loved watching at our cinema in the Victorian town of Clevedon on the Bristol Channel.

So just passing through the place where the legendary Doc Holliday died, was a real thrill.

That evening, we bade farewell to the Rockies and while we ate in the dining car our bunks were pulled out by unseen hands and made ready for the night.

Sadly, we saw nothing of Utah, as the state flashed by while we slept, and then awaking to a Nevada dawn, we again had to change our watches - but now from Mountain to Pacific Time.

We shared our breakfast table with two bearded Amish men on their way to San Francisco to sell their home-made quilts, as we journeyed on across dusty windswept Nevada plains and sage brush lands heading for the Sierra Nevada mountain range.

Our stops included Elco and Winnemucca, whose claim to fame is that its bank was robbed by Butch Cassidy back in 1900.

The snow was falling as we were served lunch looking out on yet another alpine scene, but soon we were up and over the Sierra Nevada range, via the Donnor Pass, and heading for Sacramento across sunlit green and pleasant California plains.

It was growing dark as we finally pulled into Emeryville, climbed down from the train and boarded a bus to take us over the vast Bay Bridge and at last into San Francisco, now ablaze with welcoming lights.

THE CALIFORNIA ZEPHYR

From Chicago Union
Across the USA
They rode the streamlined Zephyr
To Californ-i-a!

Left the halls of Twenties grandeur
Red-capped porters at their best
Moving luggage, guiding footsteps
Of the travellers heading West

Settled in their private cabin
In their sleek and silver train
They swapped the towers of city commerce
For the homesteads of the plain

Halting cars at level crossings
Flushing flocks from new ploughed earth
They arrowed onward, ever onward
Stretched out in their deluxe berth

On the prairie, barns and houses
Dwarfed beneath a giant sky
Lonely diners, stores and townships
Like oases flashing by

From Illinois to Iowa
The place names and the miles unroll
Then they crossed the Mississipi
Where it parts the Cereal Bowl

They hurtled t'wards a molten sunset
Hanging on the siren's tail
'Til the night brought forth the dining
Served upon the shining rail

Where seats were once, their beds appeared
One up, another down
The motion rocked them both asleep
To join each slumb'ring town

Through the dark to Omaha
Then across Nebraska's line
They gained a state and lost an hour
And watches changed to Mountain Time

They woke to scenes of cattle trails
Pockmarked with melting snow
As from behind, the wide grassland
Turning pink with dawn's rose glow

Breakfast set among such vistas
Had an extra special taste
Every mouthful, every scene shift
Seemed at once too good to waste

Then across the far horizon
Stretched the Rocky Mountains high
Snow-capped peaks of icy splendour
Reaching up to meet the sky

Apeing them - Skyscraping Denver
Mile High City of the plain
Little of its cowboy history
Shown in multi-highway lane

Next the climb to reach the mountains
Snaking slowly, surely higher
Running through the many tunnels
Blasted out with smoke and fire

Far below the raging torrents
Cutting through the chasms deep
Frozen lakes like frosted jewels
Encased in rock their waters keep

On ridges high the lonely lodges
Surrounded by the ramrod trees
Owned by those who seek the pleasure
Of the piste and swishing skis

They waited in a snow-bound siding
For a freight train heading back
Through the six-mile Moffatt tunnel
'Fore they entered in the black

After minutes in the darkness
They burst out dazzled by the light
Where skiers made a splash of colour
'Gainst the slopes of shining white

Down the lovely Fraser Canyon
Pools of water in the snow
Chasing past the wires of shadows
Going with the sunshine flow

Hoofprints on the snowy banks
Showed the paths of gentle deer
In their sanctuary of wildness
Roaming far and free from fear

214

From the blue-topped bowl of Granby
Gateway to the National Park
Out to join the Colorado
Flowing through a landscape stark

'Cross the tundra into canyons
White water crashing round huge blocks
River beaches filled with driftwood
Strewn across the tumbled rocks

Slowly wound the river's wandering
Slowly wound the track on high
Unhurried was the locomotion
Sublime the scene that passed them by

Four engines pulled the mighty Zephyr
Glimpsed on corners up ahead
As it contoured round the Rockies
Above the snaking river bed

Geese and anglers, rafts and rapids
Shared the Colorado green
Overseen by wooded hillsides
Where Indian braves could once be seen

Arid grew the land alongside
Angled cliffs towered overhead
Buzzards soared above the landscape
Picked out here in gold and red

Down the gorge to Glenwood Hot Springs
Fractured walls on either side
Here Doc Holliday lay buried
Here Fork River joined the tide

They rode through famous cowboy country
Of which the daring tales were told
And outside their picture window
The once Wild West slowly unrolled

A perpetual panaroma
Was presented to their view
Cocooned and snug in air-con comfort
While past their eyes the country flew

Now the monumental strata
Boldly carved by wind and rain
Still revered in Indian folklore
The awesome mesas of the plain

Heading for another sunset
Heading for another night
The ramparts of the Colorado
Bathed in shafts of golden light

Last to be illuminated
Last to give way to the dark
The snowtopp'd mountains as a backdrop
To the sweeping National Park

As they slept the rushing Zephyr
Powered on towards the dawn
Utah reached and then discarded
Nevada's where they'd meet the morn

Once again the clocks went back
Another state line reached and crossed
From Mountain to Pacific time
Another sixty minutes lost

Zephyr air horns blasted warnings
Signalled by a piercing light
There to stop a chance encounter
With the creatures of the night

They ate the miles with mighty ease
Pushing further to the coast
As breakfast came with bacon, eggs
Fresh fruit and crisp French toast

The double decker Zephyr
Rushed on and on full tilt
As coffee poured in dining car
And not a drop was spilt

The horizon now was bounded
By a world of scrub and sand
On the way to Winnemucca
Forging through the sage brush land

'Cross a bowl of dusty flatness
Circled round by mountains grey
The balls of tumbleweed collected
Against the fence along the way.

At a linen-covered table
Talk with bearded Amish men
For one the first ride on the railroad
And he will sure be back again

Tales of horse-drawn agriculture
Quilts and buggy trips to town
Working hard with little leisure
Farming skills still handed down

They looked out now at dust clouds swirling
Round the observation car
'Cross the salt flat desolation
Stretching westwards wide and far

Leaning poles for telegraphs
Sentinels for mile on mile
Stretching now to gambling city
Divorce and roulette Reno-style

From the neon lights and glitter
Back to river valley green
Climbing up to mountain grandeur
To a quieter, calmer scene

217

'Cross the state line in the forest
On the last lap through the pines
Past the timber homes of Truckee
Sensing ocean down the lines

Then falling snow belied the sunshine
Enjoyed below upon the plain
As if Amtrak made the weather
For its special, magic train

Through a winter wonderland
Of white-encrusted evergreens
The Zephyr ploughed on unaffected
By the snowy Christmas scenes

Then they left the high Sierra
Dropping down past deep ravine
Silently they entered gold lands
Where the spoil could still be seen

Heading now for Sacramento
Wilderness exchanged for towers
On the way the desert drabness
Swapped for brilliant green and flowers

Now the home run to the West Coast
Memories of sounds and sights
How they spanned a mighty nation
In just two full days and nights

Racing out across the wetlands
T'wards naval Portland on the bay
Lights reflected in the ocean
As the dusk wound down the day

Close now San Francisco beckoned
Its rich history to relate
Famed steep streets and Alcatraz
Framed by famous Golden Gate

They finished up at Emeryville
They'd crossed the USA
From out the Windy City
To Californ-i-a!

AMTRAK ADVENTURE – NUMBER TWO
Chicago to Los Angeles – 2,250 miles

RIDING THE TEXAS EAGLE

When Peter and I climbed aboard Amtrak's Texas Eagle, how could we have known that we'd soon be finding ourselves right in the middle of a famous Johnny Cash song.

We'd flown out to Chicago to ride this iconic Amtrak railroad all the way to Los Angeles in sunny California, with a short stopover in historic San Antonio, Texas, to visit the legendary Alamo fort,

Our 2,250-mile journey began in 'the windy city's' marble-adorned Union Station late on an April afternoon.

Soon we were ensconced in our compartment complete with comfortable seats, pull-down bunks and a small shower and toilet and out came a pack of well-worn cards, because we planned to play our highly-competitive rummy game as we watched America go by.

Again, we had stocked up with a couple of wine boxes and large packets of crisps and other nibbles to enjoy along the way.

Illinois unrolled under leaden skies with vast wheat fields and little townships flashing by, but there was a promising golden sunset as we entered the slightly-swaying dining car and found ourselves listening to a single mum's tale of woe.

Our dining companion was off to look after her invalid father, while her mother went in for a heart 'op.'

This was to be the first of many dining car tales we were to hear along the journey, giving us a fascinating insight into ordinary American life.

We sped on through St Louis and Missouri on that first night and awoke to another dawn in Arkansas with lakes, woodlands and small towns all flashing by en route for Little Rock.

It was here in the fall of 1957 that Governor Orval Faubus ordered the National Guard to prevent African-American students enrolling at the all-white Central High School.

Siren wailing, we rolled into Texas, and it was while enjoying lunch in our 'fancy dining car' that the famous Johnny Cash song, Folsom Prison Blues, came to mind.

For now, we suddenly found ourselves looking out over gleaming strands of cruelly-barbed wire into a large guarded compound with groups of inmates standing around.

So was this Folsom Prison, we wondered.

In the song, Cash's lifer hears the train's lonesome whistle and wishes he could move down the line away from this place of his life-long incarceration.

Unfortunately for this travel piece, this place of detention was not Folsom Prison, which we discovered, was in California, our destination state.

However, in the song, the train does goes travelling 'on down to San Antone' and so was our Texas Eagle, but not before we'd rumbled slowly through towering skyscraper Dallas.

For most older readers, the very name Dallas can only be synonymous with the shock assassination of President John F Kennedy as his motorcade drove through the city back in November, 1963.

We left the train in San Antonio and enjoyed a memorable afternoon visiting the Alamo, an 18th-century Spanish mission, now preserved as a museum, which marks the infamous 1836 battle for Texan independence from Mexico.

After staying overnight, we spent the following day wandering along the San Antonio River walk, now a landmark promenade lined with cafes and shops, and ascended the Tower of the Americas for a bird's eye view over the city before catching the next train bound for Los Angeles.

It was dark when we climbed onboard our second Eagle and awoke to a far more barren landscape, punctuated by a series of green river valleys, until even those dried up and we journeyed ever onward over barren scrubland, while vultures circled in a pale blue sky.

That lunchtime, we shared our dining table with two talkative middle-aged sisters, who both happened to be widows, on their way to an evangelical conference, who asked us to join them in a prayer when the food arrived.

Needless to say, we gained a fascinating insight into their lives and enjoyed a most convivial afternoon as the time and the miles flashed by.

Later in the day, a range of distant peaks, shrouded in clouds, hove into sight and quite suddenly, the weather changed and rain splattering on the domed observation car windows obscured the view.

Our Eagle made a brief halt in the small town of Alpine, Texas, which is surrounded by distant peaks and is the gateway to a national park and here we had to move our watches forward an hour to Mountain Time.

Now rolling hills and open prairie grasslands were stretching ahead as far as the eye could see and we'd entered prime cattle-rearing country of the old West bound for El Paso.

This historic city, established in pioneering days alongside the banks of the Rio Grande, is close to the Mexican border and the Franklin Mountains State Park, home to cacti and desert wildlife, including coyotes and golden eagles.

From El Paso, we journeyed steadily on into New Mexico, waiting patiently in the occasional siding for quarter-mile-long freight trains to go rolling by, and then forward into Arizona, now time for dinner.

While breakfasting in our dining car the following morning, our Eagle passed stockyards full of shuffling cattle.

Now we were crossing classic Arizona desert-like landscape, punctuated by sandstone peaks, en route for old Fort Yuma, where a white man killed an Apache Chief and started a war.

223

The Apaches planned to sneak into the fort dressed as federal soldiers, so massacred a supply column to steal the uniforms, but one man managed to escape and made it back to the fort to raise the alarm.

Approaching journey's end, we passed through Palm Springs, the famous Southern Californian city in the Sonoran Desert, known for its, hot springs, stylish hotels, golf courses and spas.

Now back on Pacific Time, we moved on through grassy foothills and fruit-filled orchards to come at last to Los Angeles Union Station with its impressive halls of marble and glass.

Next stop was booking into an hotel in Hollywood, the famous town of movie stars, for a couple of days' sightseeing before flying home again, including visiting Venice Beach and the J. Paul Getty Museum's Getty Center, perched on a hilltop.

Since writing this piece we've discovered that the Texas Eagle no longer runs direct from Chicago to Los Angeles, but passengers can still cross the country to LA on the South West Chief calling en route at Santa Fe, Williams, Grand Canyon National Park and Flagstaff.

THE TEXAS EAGLE

They flew back 12 months later
A new goal on their mind
To LA now via Texas
Chicago left behind

As out from Union Station
The loco pulled away
Their journey lay before them
Ahead the USA

Their Zephyr now an Eagle
Part of the Amtrak fleet
Leaving sidings in their wake
And crowded city street

Skyscrapers disappearing
Behind the urban sprawl
Once more they heard the siren's
Mournful, haunting call

Settled in there starts the card game
Out comes the wine box then the snacks
Dealing hands of friendly rummy
As they shift along the tracks

Illinois unrolling
Beneath a leaden sky
Refineries and lorry parks
And scrapyards passing by

Glistening strips of tarmac
Great trucks immersed in spray
Pounding through the wheatfields
Towards the end of day

Little townships linked by rails
Snaking 'cross the dark'ning land
While cutting through the lowering grey
Beamed the sunset's orange band

Over dinner tales of journeys
Why they came and where they go
Beautiful the single mother
Spilling out her family's woe

Heading South to see her parents
Her mother's heart due for an op
Strong father's neck now triply broken
With them both she'll have to stop

Mexican the landscape gardener
Crossed the border – ne'er return
His sights now turning to Chicago
If more dollars he can earn

Into Missouri speeds the train now
St Louis city reached at night
Its spirit reaching ever skyward
With an archway etched in light.

Cabin quickly turned to bedroom
Bunks made up and sheets turned back
Up the steps and strapped in safely
Like hand luggage on a rack

In the night the creaks and rattles
Magnified as others sleep
Rocked by the continual motion
As across the miles they leap

In the homesteads passed in darkness
In children's bedrooms scattered round
Do they fire imagination
With the Amtrak's siren sound?

A new day dawns in Arkansas
En route now to Little Rock
Its name still steeped in infamy
That engendered worldwide shock

Far behind them lakes in Winter
Closing now on bursting Spring
Cherry trees in pink haze blossom
Making hope and heart take wing

And yet their journey has a shadow
Explaining why they were delayed
On the track a soul despairing
Sadly down a life was laid

Creeks and lakes and green-tipped woodland
Hem the rails on either side
Opening then to grazing pastures
Above an eagle – wings spread wide

Then the swamplands draped in purple
Egrets wading 'neath the gaze
Of raptors circling ever higher
While in their lounge the travellers laze

Calves just racing for the pleasure
While mothers feed on fresh, sweet grass
Scenes of rural contemplation
Outside the windows swiftly pass

Another hamlet filled with glimpses
Of other peoples, other ways
School buses waiting for their charges
Who gaily greet the lengthening days

They crossed the line at Texarkana
Entering the Lone Star State
The faded Ritz Motel a witness
To seedy life and secret date

The run-down station had a sign there
It said the city's Twice As Nice
But in the neighbouring prison compound
The inmates stared with eyes of ice

Behind the fence of silver barbed wire
In groups or singly there they stood
One gave the train the single finger
His farewell wave was all but good

In the woodland new leaf bursting
White blossom bright among the green
Turning swamp to sylvan beauty
Giving glades a vibrant sheen

Wild wisteria garlands trackside
Exuberant in its natural state
More at home in free profusion
Than trained to frame a garden gate

Past graveyards filled with Southern flowers
Past scrapyards filled with Southern cars
Piled in heaps of crumpled metal
Detritus of the Stripes and Stars

Lunching then on salmon seared
With happy sisters saying Grace
Joined together with their Christ now
After one had seen Death's face

A life of husbands, drink and drugging
Discarded now for her own good
Descendant of a pioneer, she's
Finally living as she should

Now the fields give way to streets
Brash Dallas fills the April sky
'Cross 40 years the echoes come
Here JFK did cruelly die

Mirrored blocks he never saw
Not built before the day he fell
Where are now the dreams he wove?
For some they still retain their spell

After miles of factory silos
Smoking tower and storage shed
Back to rolling, peaceful pasture
Filling vistas far ahead

Now in meadows clumps of cacti
As the further South they go
All too soon the shadows lengthen
Light takes on a molten glow

As night rolls in, distant horizon
Retaining still the sun's gold fire
While above light blue to navy
Darkens sky o'er day's bright pyre

In San Antone they broke their journey
City of the Alamo
Here the heroes lost the battle
But in dying beat their foe

Along the river tamed in concrete
Tourist bustle 'neath the trees
Terrace cafes, arching bridges
Jazz and birdsong on the breeze

Back aboard the Texas Eagle
Even though the hour was late
Ready to resume their journey
Out across the dark'ned state

From the green of river valleys
Through the scrubland now they pound
Where the cream of yucca flowers
Punctuates the sandy ground

Overhead the vultures circling
Black against the wide blue sky
While below the long train passes
Over river beds bone dry

Del Rio gives a chance for smokers
To stretch their legs along the track
Lighting up with urgent action
Before attendants call them back

Palm trees mixed with ramrod poplars
Where US touches Mexico
Then the recreation area
Where lakes within the desert show

Ahead the names that live in legend
El Paso, Tucson down the line
Home to boyhood cowboy heroes
Their image branded on their time

In the parched and empty landscape
A sudden movement takes the eye
Three deer disturbed from peaceful grazing
From the man-made monster fly

Red-tipped stalks of flowering cactus
Before the crossing of ravine
On the towering Pacos High Bridge
Far below the river green

Through sandstone cuttings driving on
Ever-edged by trackside wire
Amid the rock-strewn barren wasteland
A cactus bursts in blossom fire

Yellow blooms and purple flowers
Thanks to all the Springtime rain
Line the route past rocky gulches
As the lunch is served again

Table talk with lady farmer
Travelling now because she could
Next to her a trainee film girl
Heading out to Hollywood

Then from out the desert flatness
Rise the mountains stark and proud
Dappled now with stripes of sunlight
Filtered through the thickening cloud

Rollercoaster ridge in profile
Etched against a sky of blue
As the distant peaks are shrouded
And the rain obscures the view

Who can bemoan the change in weather
As the windows streak with drops
The colour's there because of water
They just hope it quickly stops

In the lounge a plucky lady
Round trip journey near complete
Armed with crosswords and her rations
Sleeping in a budget seat.

A brief halt in Alpine, Texas
Gateway to the Big Bend Park
Changing here to Mountain Timescale
One hour closer to the dark

Rolling hills and open grassland
Stretching far as eye can see
All around prime cattle country
Prairies of West history

Vast tracts of land with ghosts a –plenty
Running on to El Paso
Warrior Indians riding mustangs
Cowboys taming wild bronco

Freight train traffic heading Eastward
Brings their progress to a stand
Time to savour now the stillness
Of this sea of scrub and sand

Silence broken by the rumble
Union Pacific wagons roll
Containers shipped across the oceans
Hauled by diesel now not coal

From El Paso farewell to Texas
New Mexico now lies ahead
Then to enter Arizona
Time for dinner then to bed

On a hillside o'er El Paso
Outlined in lights a giant lone star
Shining out the pride of statehood
Visible from near and far

In the rail cars, children playing
People talking, while some sleep
Warmly curling under blankets
Counting miles instead of sheep

In the morning in the desert
Saugauro cactus standing tall
Arms aloft to greet the new day
And to catch the rare rainfall

Past stockyards filled with shuffling cattle
Past massive walls of golden hay
An immigrant who built a business
The signs proclaiming McElhay

Breakfast with a farmer's son
Who turned to teaching musically
A rail trip now his dream vacation
From hard graft running B&B

Under peaks of sandstone starkness
Curves the train around a bend
The desert merging into scrubland
Seemingly without an end

On a bluff at old Fort Yuma
Indian church with walls of cream
Looks across the cultivation
Oasis in the desert scene

From the dry and sandy dullness
To the edge of Salton Sea
Pleasant looking by the date palms
Yet death to fish and you and me

Into Palm Springs through the palm trees
Then past towers shining white
Farming wind with giant propellers
On the plains and mountain height

Meet a black cap-wearing artist
His Dutch descent here all too clear
Unpacking now his well-used sketch pad
Like a latter-day Vermeer

Now they passed by grassy foothills
Orchards filled with orange fruit
Heading coastwards through vast suburbs
Drawn behind the loco's toot

Journey's end at Union Station
Halls of marble, wood and glass
Echoes here of Thirties glamour
Where the movie stars did pass

Back again in California
Once more clocks show Pacific Time
LA waiting there to greet them
Come on in, the weather's fine.

THE OTHER WAYS

Besides all the walks described in this book, we have of course, completed many other long-distance trails, but sadly these were in the days before I started writing about them.

I guess my rationale at the time was that if I spent my working days writing press releases for all my PR clients, why on Earth should I want to carry on writing while walking?

So, while these walks are not featured here, we feel they still rate a mention and perhaps the most important of them is The Greater Ridgeway, described by Ray Quinlan and published as a Cicerone guide.

This fabulous walk runs for 363 miles all the way from Lyme Regis in Dorset to Hunstanton in Norfolk, incorporating four linking national trails, the Wessex Ridgeway, the Ridgeway National Trail, the Icknield Way and the Peddars Way.

It is a walk of huge variation from the undulating Dorset hills and the wide-open plateau of Salisbury Plain, forward to the open ridges above Wantage in Oxfordshire and the lofty heights of Ivinghoe Beacon, in Buckinghamshire, and thence forward to the Thetford Forest beyond Cambridge and Newmarket.

Needless to say, we had many small adventures along the way, including staying in a magnificent manor house in Dorset and meeting an elderly retired society photographer, who had snapped a picture of the former King Edward VIII and Mrs Simpson at Quaglino's Restaurant in London.

We climbed up onto Salisbury Plain in a blizzard with guns from the Army ranges booming away in the distance and later left a coin in Waylands Smithy, the Neolithic site near the Uffington White Horse, so that our boots would always remain shod.

And on another occasion we stayed with a millionaire, who had opened his home to paying guests because he enjoyed the company, and he celebrated his Scottish roots by cooking us haggis for breakfast.

Memories, like these, stand out like small beacons in one's mind long after the details of a particular walk have faded into the past and so it was with the136-mile long and circular Shropshire Way, which features in another Cicerone guide.

This is a particularly attractive walk that starts and finishes close to the River Severn in historic Shrewsbury and links small and picturesque market towns with pretty villages on its rural round.

We were booked in to a large roadside inn on our second night and arrived weary and ready for a pint, a hearty meal and a good night's rest.

But alas, this hostelry had changed hands after our booking and the new owners had taken over that very day and were not expecting any guests, because they were closed for a refurbishment!

But they rose to the challenge finding us a room and locating two gammon steaks in a freezer, which they cooked for our supper, and when I carelessly left one of my walking poles behind, they kindly mailed it back to me.

On another evening we arrived in the small west Shropshire market town of Clun and stepped out from our B&B for a bite to eat in a nearby Inn,

It happened to be Quiz Night and all the regulars were in a boisterous and merry mood, which was really the last thing we two weary walkers needed, but they insisted we join in and would not take no for an answer.

Was this our mischievous Cosmic Joker striking again, I wondered, but, no, because Lady Luck was at hand.

We were not doing too badly, we thought, and then came a 15-point section on 1960s pop stars and, of course, being our era, we could answer almost every one and to our amazement we won!

"So now we can call ourselves the Quiz Masters of Clun," said Peter.

Walking the, often wild, Offa's Dyke trail, covering 177 mostly spectacular miles from Chepstow on the River Severn all the way to Prestatyn in North Wales, was one of our early trekking highlights.

Many memories from this, including the time we sat on a snowy hillside and arranged over a mobile phone call for Channel Four to feature Hollywood star John Malkovich having breakfast with Cardiff secretaries at our client, Cosmo Fry's Big Sleep Hotel.

And also, on another snowy day, being offered a lift by a bus driver as we sat having our mid-morning coffee under a hedgerow and airily declining his kind offer as "we are walkers".

You will recall how all the massive construction works for HS2 so rudely interrupted our progress while walking the Heart of England Way; well, we experienced a comparable situation with a twist while walking the North Downs Way many years earlier.

This wonderful 130-mile walk follows the higher ground between the market town of Farnham in Surrey and Dover on the Kent coast, taking in the Surrey Hills and the Kent Downs.

We were using quite an old OS map, produced before the Eurotunnel rail link forged its way across the Kent landscape, and suddenly found ourselves on a lane, which no longer registered with the landscape around us!

Needless to say, the penny dropped instantly, but it took us quite some time to extricate ourselves from the situation and get back on course.

The North Downs Way finishes in Dover, but as we had already ticked off that destination on our alternative Southern coast-to-coast walk, we decided instead to follow a linking trail and finish in Canterbury and visit its famous cathedral.

Sadly, it was not our tour of this magnificent edifice, where Thomas Becket was murdered by knights for defying King Henry II, which stands out in my memory, but the annoying fact that we had our evening dinner starter and main course in one busy town centre restaurant and our dessert in another!

The food in the first eatery was so poor that we voted with our feet and quickly found somewhere much more conducive for our sweet.

Having completed the North Downs Way, our next step was naturally to set out on its neighbouring companion, the South Downs Way, which runs for one hundred miles high above the South Coast from Eastbourne to Winchester.

Overnighting at a B&B just off the seafront in Eastbourne prompted a personal deja vu moment for Peter, because the house once belonged to his great uncle and he used to spend his childhood summer holidays there.

The following day, as a stark reminder of the need to pay attention, one missed signpost led us miles out of our way, added hours to our day's walk and at one point had me hoisting Peter over a barbed-wire fence to regain the trail that lay invitingly on the other side.

Our Cicerone guide gave us the choice of walking either eastbound or westbound on the South Downs Way and we chose the latter because psychologically, it seemed more comfortable to be walking towards home.

But this turned out to be the wrong decision because we completed the trail in two halves in Spring and Summer, both coinciding with periods of high winds, against which we had to struggle up and down hill as we made our way ever westward.

Most sensible walkers choose to walk from west to east, so taking advantage of the prevailing westerly winds, we were told.

So, I think that after all these years and miles of walking, our Cosmic Joker had the very last laugh!

MORE TALES FROM THE TRAILS

You will have read by now of our Cosmic Joker, who has already made several guest appearances in this narrative, and is always ready to hold us to account if we step too far out of line.

A classic example of this was the late afternoon we arrived, tired and ready for a rest, at a beautiful manor house somewhere in the middle section of our Weston-super-Mare to Dover trek.

To our surprise, there were several peacocks pecking about on a beautifully-manicured lawn and when our lady hostess answered the door, she explained they were her pets.

She welcomed us in and as she was leading us up the stairs, she turned and said she'd decided we could have separate rooms, but one was much larger than the other, so we'd have to make the choice.

"He can have the small one," I heard myself say and the Cosmic Joker heard it too.

Peter's room wasn't really small at all and as she led me to my door, she turned and said: "I've been painting the window sills in here and I'm afraid it still smells!"

I suppose it must be inevitable that when any two friends spend time together over the years a camaraderie develops based on shared experiences and so it has been for Peter and I.

Funnily enough it was on the last stage of this walk along the coast towards Dover that one particular phrase entered our folklore.

It was a busy Saturday night and we'd managed to secure the last table in a packed Italian restaurant and when the waitress came to take our order, we asked if we might play cards at our table.

We always play rummy between courses and have always done so over our trekking years, but normally ask our host if that is OK, out of courtesy. unless of course we happen to be frequenting an inn.

"Oh! I don't know, so I'll go and ask," the girl replied. A few moments later the obviously-harassed proprietor appeared and we repeated our request.

"I have been running this restaurant for many years and never before have I had such a request, so I think not!" came his response.

Needless to say that over the years certain situations have occurred when a decision is required from one or other of us and has prompted the response:" I think not!"

On another memorable occasion after our California Zephyr ride to San Francisco, we were walking down a sunny side street jam packed with parked cars from nose to tail when we came upon a gap by a high wooden gate.

Here a large notice in bold black letters declared: 'Do not obstruct these gate...not even slightly!' So, yes, we use the response: 'not even slightly,' when the situation demands.

One afternoon during the time that Peter and I worked together at my former Media-Consult news PR agency in the North Somerset village of Wrington, a highly- delighted client called to congratulate him for landing his company on the front page of his trade magazine.

"Oh, that's appeared has it," Peter replied in a matter of fact way because he'd done that job and moved on, which prompted the never-to-be-forgotten response: "Peter, how can you be so disinterested?!"

Further digressing from the trail for a moment, I well remember the morning in the office when I declared that I'd never work for a double-glazing company, because I could not think of anything more boring.

Sure enough the Cosmic Joker was listening because some years later I found myself doing exactly that and it wasn't at all boring.

Returning to the trail, there was the morning on the Severn Way when we came down to breakfast at our Bridgnorth hotel to discover there was smoked salmon and scrambled eggs on the menu, which is a particular favourite.

Alas, when the dish arrived, the eggs had been well and truly overcooked to now resemble a jumble of pale, yellow balls.

Surprise, surprise, the following morning at our hotel in Bewdley a further 16 miles down the river, this dish was again on the menu and we explained to the waitress that if we could have a portion of soft scrambled egg with the smoked salmon on the side, then that would be much appreciated.

Sadly, the chef, clearly had his or her own idea as to how this dish should be presented, for when it arrived, it appeared as if a bowl had been lined with salmon with the scrambled eggs poured in on top and then turned upside-down on the plate,

The result was two large bombes with the hot egg continuing to cook the salmon, so giving off the aroma of steamed fish.

That afternoon as we walked wearily into Worcester in the pouring rain, Peter said that, even if smoked salmon and scrambled eggs were on the menu the following morning, he was going to decline them.

Our Cosmic Joker must have been listening because sure enough, when we came down to breakfast said dish was again listed and Peter was being asked to stick to his resolution or 'eat his words.'

He decided to 'eat his words' so we explained to the very helpful waitress how we liked our dish presented.

"Oh! I am sure our chef can oblige, but I'll go and ask," she said. She was back two minutes later with the news: "We're out of smoked salmon!"

Now some readers may take the view that with so much starvation in the world, surely this pair should simply think themselves lucky to have such a choice and indeed I also feel that way and am grateful for it.

When having breakfast on the trail we always ask for two pieces of toast and not a rack-full because we know the rest will end up in the bin, which is such a terrible waste!

On a lighter note, we arrived at one inn at 5pm on a winter afternoon while walking the Macmillan Way to find the place locked and a notice telling us this hostelry would not be opening until 6pm.

So it was time for our oft-used Plan B and we settled ourselves in the nearby parish church porch and were soon cloaked in darkness.

Peter suggested that we pass the time by my singing some of the Irish folk songs I know by heart and I willingly obliged, but then we spotted a couple hurrying past and goodness knows what they must have thought!

I have always enjoyed singing and Peter is happy to join me in a ritual, which always takes place every time we walk through a long canal tunnel or under a wide motorway bridge.

I can't remember when we started taking advantage of the excellent acoustics they provide, but our chosen song is always the Frank Ifield classic, I Remember You, including a little yodelling.

Tradition insists that we start with the line - And stars that fell like the rain out of the blue - and we finish when we reach the end of the tunnel or bridge underpass, even if we are in mid-verse!

JOURNEY'S END – FOR NOW

Walking the highways and byways of Britain, roughly every twelve weeks or so over the past forty-odd years, has been a rich and, completely separate thread, weaving its way through the tapestry of our lives.

It started, as I explained earlier, when we both had young families, and is still continuing now that we are grandparents, Peter currently in his 80th year and me in my 76th.

As you may have already noted, I start every walk by asking "I wonder what adventures we shall have today."

These adventures come in many forms, from fascinating conversations with the interesting people we have met, to losing our way on countless occasions and to all the acts of kindness shown to us along life's highway.

Britain is probably the only country in the world with such a vast network of footpaths close to towns and villages just waiting for everyone to use them.

But ironically, we often walk for hours and hours without meeting anyone, except maybe the occasional dog walkers near habitations and this rather shatters the illusion that Britain is built-up and over-crowded,

The amazing fact is that only around two per cent of the landmass is urbanised, when not including large gardens and green urban spaces, and there are miles and miles of open country for everyone to get out and enjoy.

Of course, not every walk is without hitches, even with a highly-experienced duo, such as Peter and myself.

The list of items left at home or misplaced en route includes anoraks, fleeces, gloves, walking poles, flasks, both empty or full of coffee or hot chocolate, sandwiches, biscuits, cakes, maps, guide books and not forgetting or rather actually forgetting, boots.

On one occasion Peter had left his trusty Scarpa boots at home and had to buy a pair of expensive close-fitting Wellington boots by a well-known maker.

After 16 miles on uneven footpaths and roadways, his feet were par-boiled with every tiny stone producing a sharp pain and I had difficulty extracting him from the offending footwear that evening in our hotel.

Then there was the time when we returned from Welshpool after completing a section of the Cross Britain Way and Peter discovered that his boots were not in the boot – of his car that is.

Calls were made to the police in the town and the hotel, where we had been picked up by taxi, but it was the wife of the said driver, who unearthed the boots in his boot.

Peter was eventually reunited with his Scarpas, but not before some postal delay, all of which prompted the following poem.

BOOTS AWAY

My boots are made for walking
Not stuck in far Welshpool
So when I couldn't find them
I felt a careless fool
I thought I might have left them
On hotel's outside chair
But when they went to check for me
My boots they were not there
I asked the taxi driver
He said he'd have a look
Insurance claim would need police
To have it in their book
But then the driver's missus
Gave me the welcome news
She'd found the boots within the boot
No walks for me in shoes
She said that she would post them
But they did not appear
My joy at their discovery
Was turning now to fear

Nige said: Just get a new pair
I found some on the net
Together with some gaiters
Ideal when it is wet
The price it was a bargain
But then a nasty shock
An e-mail from supplier
"Your boots are out of stock."
A further call to Welshpool
Revealed my boots were back
It seemed address had washed off
When out the postie's sack
Once more within a parcel
My boots they headed home
In time to be re-polished
And off again to roam.
In future I'll look after them
It's only me to blame
And yomps in carpet slippers
Are never quite the same.

Peter has been writing his Betjemanesque-style poetry virtually ever
since we began walking together and his two Let The Good Rhymes Roll
anthologies are available from Amazon.

He often finds his inspiration on our walks from some small incident,
which happens along the way, or maybe a stunning view we have
stopped to admire.

My inspiration for walking derives from one small incident, which occurred while my much-loved Auntie Lil was taking my four-year-old self for yet another walk across Bristol's Durdham Downs.

"Auntie, Auntie, can we go back now because my legs are aching and my feet are hurting?" I pleaded.

"No," she said. "Come along, come along. Pick your feet up, because walking is good for you!"
"

Me with Auntie Lil on Weston-super-Mare Promenade

USEFUL INFORMATION

Whenever we set off on our walks, we make sure we have the detailed guide book covering the route and the appropriate Landranger OS maps.

The books are essential for giving mileages, when working out overnight accommodation and lunch stops, and for following the path when marker signs are missing or have been obscured.

The maps are essential for seeing where you are at all times in relation to the landscape and also for organising diversions where necessary, because of weather conditions or unforeseen factors, such as the intrusion of the HS2 rail project.

As you will see elsewhere, we have used a number of Cicerone guide books for our walks over the years and have found them all to be excellent - www.cicerone.co.uk

For our two cross-Britain walks, from Boston in Lincolnshire to Abbotsbury in Dorset and from Boston to Barmouth in North Wales, we followed superb guides published by the Macmillan Way Association - www.macmillanway.org

And all our canal adventures have been completed using J.M. Pearson & Son Ltd's Canal Companions - www.jmpearson.co.uk

The success of a walk, no matter how breathtaking the scenery, is also determined by the quality of the overnight accommodation.

This needs to be located as close as possible to the route and allowing achievable distances between the stages, especially during the shorter daylight hours of winter months.

Over the years we have experienced a huge variety of city and country accommodation, from B&Bs and pubs to hotels.

For the latter, we have regularly found Premier Inns - www.premierinn.com - to be an ideal choice, often conveniently close to the footpath, especially in the case of canals, and with spacious and comfortable en-suite bedrooms and ever-helpful staff.

Now to your essential equipment - thankfully not too much:

First your rucksack: we use the 70-litre size, which we find can contain all we need for overnight stops, appropriate clothing for the prevailing conditions, including wet weather gear, and vacuum flask and water bottle. A waterproof liner is also essential, as we discovered during our initial soggy outing on the West Highland Way.

Next your boots: choose a size large enough for you to wear a thin inner sock and an outer thicker sock and make sure you have worn the boots in before attempting a walk of any significant distance. Peter, as you will see from his poem on Page 151, wears Scarpa Delta GTX Boots – www.scarpa.co.uk, while Nigel wears a wider fit Altberg hiking boot - www.altberg.co.uk

They need to be re-polished with waterproof wax after every outing. Peter uses Leather Genie Balsam - www.leathergenie.co.uk – but other brands, as they say, are available.

Wet weather gear: A roomy anorak. We wear Rohan Ascent Jackets - www.rohan.co.uk. Waterproof trousers – as you will see from Peter's poem on Page 83, we like Rohan's Dry Requisite Trousers, which spare you the on-off dance with the plastic versions. Gaiters, which keep your lower trouser legs mud-free and dry when walking through wet grass, Waterproof gloves.

Walking poles: These should be adjustable and preferably not the Nordic walking variety. And we use two poles, which gives us extra stability in uneven and muddy conditions.

A small first aid kit for insect bites, blisters and small cuts and grazes, which might become infected if left untreated.

Head torch: Useful when the daylight fades on winter walks and when negotiating canal tunnels.

Map case: Large enough to hold the guide book or map.

Mobile phone plus charger: Handy for using Google Maps to provide exact directions to a pub or overnight stop, contacting a taxi firm for the end of walk pick-up and for taking pictures to record special scenes along the way.

And finally, a large, foldable sheet of sturdy plastic, useful for when sitting on damp or muddy ground for a coffee and cake or lunch stop.

To the above you can, of course, add a compass for use on moorland and high open spaces, where paths can be difficult to follow and it is easy to become disorientated in misty weather.